# New Rules for
# Radicals:
# TNT for Faith-Based Leaders

## Techniques and Tactics

### WILLARD W. C. ASHLEY SR.

JUDSON PRESS
PUBLISHERS SINCE 1824
VALLEY FORGE, PA

New Rules for Radicals: TNT for Faith-Based Leaders
© 2021 by Judson Press, Valley Forge, PA 19482-0851
All rights reserved.

Judson Press has made every effort to trace the ownership of all quotes. In the event of a question arising from the use of a quote, we regret any error made and will be pleased to make the necessary correction in future printings and editions of this book.

Bible quotations in this volume are from the New Revised Standard Version of the Bible, copyright © 1989 by the Division of Christian Education of the National Council of the Churches of Christ in the United States of America. Used by permission. All rights reserved. And from *The Holy Bible*, King James Version.

Interior design by Lisa Cain.
Cover design by Danny Ellison.

Library of Congress Cataloging-in-Publication data

Cataloging-in-Publication Data available upon request.
Library of Congress Cataloging-in-Publication Data

Names: Ashley, Williard W. C. Sr., author.
Title: New rules for radicals : TNT for faith-based leaders / Williard W.
    C. Ashley, Sr.
Description: Valley Forge, PA : Judson Press, 2021. | Includes
    bibliographical references and index.
Identifiers: LCCN 2021011247 (print) | LCCN 2021011248 (ebook) | ISBN
    9780817018269 (paperback) | ISBN 9780817082291 (epub)
Subjects: LCSH: Leadership--Religious aspects--Christianity. | Christianity
    and culture. | Christianity and justice. | Social justice--Religious
    aspects--Christianity.
Classification: LCC BV4597.53.L43 A84 2021  (print) | LCC BV4597.53.L43
    (ebook) | DDC 261/.1--dc23
LC record available at https://lccn.loc.gov/2021011247
LC ebook record available at https://lccn.loc.gov/2021011248

Printed in the U.S.A.

First printing, 2021.

# CONTENTS

Foreword                                                                    *iv*

Introduction                                                                *ix*

**Chapters**

1   Context: Know Your Setting                                          *1*

2   Conflict: Embrace Conflict as Part of the
     Process for Change                                   *27*

3   Charisma: Use Your Gifts                                            *51*

4   Commitment: Agree to Engage                                         *65*

5   Competence: Do Your Homework, Learn,
     Train, and Network                                   *83*

6   Creativity: Have Fun Winning
     by Being Unpredictable                               *99*

7   Celebration: Build on Your Wins                                     *113*

8   Character: The War Has Just Begun                                   *127*

Afterword                                                                   *145*

Additional Resources                                                        *149*

# FOREWORD

*New Rules for Radicals* is a must-read for those who believe in and are committed to the possibility of a racially and socially just society. For all of us working on the front lines to uplift humanity, it is food for the mind, spirit, and soul.

This book deepens the historical work of Saul Alinsky and the Industrial Areas Foundation community organizing model by adding an anti-racist, systemic analysis that is pivotal to community development and empowerment. In Saul Alinsky's *Rules for Radicals*, his tactics for organizing are good. However, they are rooted in winning the struggles around issues as the goal and not in addressing what causes the issues. Alternatively, in *New Rules for Radicals*, Willard Ashley Sr. clarifies that equity in housing, health care, employment, and the many other issues affecting marginalized communities, cannot be achieved by confronting each individual problem alone. Dr. Ashley clarifies that winning the issue must be accompanied by the understanding that the cause of the issue is structural racism, and that the ultimate elimination of structural racism must be the ultimate goal for community organizing for racial and social justice.

Dr. Ashley uses his God-given authority to define what it means to be a faith-based radical for social change. He presents us with an unembellished demystification of the word "radical" and its meaning within a faith-centered context. If you are a faith-based leader or community organizer and you do not identify yourself as a radical, this book will inspire

you to claim that identity with honor! Dr. Ashley acknowledges our humanity, the struggles and pain we encounter as
anti-racist faith-based leaders and community organizers,
and the necessity of developing the skills to effectively and
consistently counteract those realities. I am given hope by
the very idea that Dr. Ashley wrote *New Rules for Radicals*
to assist us in identifying areas where our fatigue would lead
us to believe that change for a just society can never happen.
The infusion of encouragement and new pathways for change
on our journey to social justice is always a welcome and
necessary addition to our toolbox for community organizing.

I always listen to Will because I recognize and respect
his brilliance, years of dedication as an anti-racist community organizer, and deeply held commitment to building an
anti-racist movement for social justice. These might not be
enough credentials for some folks to listen to and believe
Willard Ashley. But he also carries the academic credentials
and qualifications to match his organizing experience—
MDiv, DMin, SCP, NCPsyA, and CGP among them. Therefore, one cannot help but respect, appreciate, and applaud
the combination of his community organizing resume and
academic credentials.

For social justice advocates, Dr. Ashley's experience and
expertise offer a model for community organizing that
provides a holistic and spiritually healthy process and gener-
ates the integration of our faith with an anti-racist analysis.
He challenges us to be less bureaucratic and more relational,
and he acknowledges the multiplicities and complications
of the mixed identities we carry in our work as faith-based
leaders and community organizers. As organizers, we often
say we wear many hats without fully acknowledging the
personal, spiritual, mental, and professional costs these
many hats carry. At times, these hats overlap and even get
in the way of each other; yet, together, they represent who
we are. Dr. Ashley models this for us by sharing his personal

experiences as a pastor, therapist, and anti-racist community organizer, and he provides us with a path to becoming healthier, happier, and more effective in our work as social justice advocates.

*New Rules for Radicals* is simply genius. It offers us a well-thought-out blueprint for doing this work in the presence of a toxic and unhealthy societal culture. While many of us recognize that we work and live in a culture that does not provide life, liberty, and the pursuit of happiness for all, this book is a testament to the possibility that we can walk in purpose and practice care and harmony within our work as faith-based social justice leaders. It is a reminder that we must go back and reconnect with the wonderful memories of our elders' wisdom and survival skills.

This book could not have come at a better time. Being part of the current social justice movement is both life-giving and fatiguing—exacerbated by the personal losses and inequities highlighted by the COVID-19 pandemic. In that context, Dr. Ashley reminds us that we need some new rules; the old ones are not enough. He also reminds us that our words and the spaces we occupy as change agents have power and can define, direct, redirect, or destroy the social justice work we are committed to. He points out the potential seductiveness and divisiveness that can happen in our work when we are overly cautious and not open to new ways of thinking. Dr. Ashley proposes that we learn from our sacred texts, and from the daily practices and social realities that support our work.

Like many of my colleagues, I forget that social justice work takes a toll on our physical, psychological, spiritual, personal, and social lives. *New Rules for Radicals* challenges us to better recognize that we have the right and responsibility to take care of ourselves so that we can take care of those we love as we work to change the world. Dr. Ashley reminds us that healing is a necessary process for the communities we serve—as well as for ourselves—in the work of social justice. He also reminds us that we suffer from the same hurt and damage that our communities do.

The stories and examples that Dr. Ashley shares in this book are funny, loving, sometimes scary, and always have profound meaning in how we do our work for social justice. Reading this book helped me personally acknowledge and recognize the impact the years of social justice work has had, and is still having, on every aspect of my life. *New Rules for Radicals* presents tools that can help all of us create space in our lives to expand our knowledge in becoming more effective community organizers.

To my co-hearts in the Movement: This book is a critical resource for our survival on our journey to building a socially and racially just society.

To Dr. Ashley: Thank you for your work in the community, and for caring enough about the rest of us to share your love, learnings, and knowledge with us.

Peace and Blessings to my good brother, Dr. Will Ashley Sr., and to those who read this fantastic book!

—**Barbara Crain Major**
Anti-Racist Community Organizer

# INTRODUCTION

## Four Questions Radicals Ask

There are three cultural responses to public challenges: service, mobilization, and organizing. In Chapter 4, I will explain all three models. This book aims to equip communities and congregations to have a voice to effect change in systems, institutions, organizations, policies, practices, and laws.

COVID-19 put the world on hold. Americans experienced record unemployment rates. Worldwide protests happened in the aftermath of the killing of unarmed Black men and women at the hands of the police. Three accomplished Black women started Black Lives Matter[1] in 2013. During the COVID-19 pandemic Black Lives Matter took center stage. In years past, America sat silent as the BLM movement was mischaracterized and demonized. The realities of racial disparities during the pandemic gave renewed credibility and global support to BLM. In response to this newfound energy against racism, angry, radicalized white supremacists heard a dog whistle that violence at their hands is acceptable. The systems intended to protect all US citizens, build a strong economy, and provide health care for the sick failed.

Citizens shouted cries of moral outrage. The former president of the United States of America, Barack Obama, warned

New Rules for Radicals

people not to repeat this cycle of being angry now and two weeks later operating as usual.[2] The planet is crying out for people of goodwill to act; we have no choice if we want a future. Mainstream America's romance with apathy, indifference, and complacency is not acceptable. The purpose of this book is to offer tools, strategies, and stories to give you hope. Organized citizens can win!

Americans have faced widespread polarization, intimidation, manipulation, and alienation. Various voices from across the United States of America are calling for the return of the days of civility, compassion, conversation, collaboration, creativity, courage, and character. We have entered an era whereby many of our leaders receive an "A" for charm and an "F" for compassion and courage. God calls leaders and citizens to a higher bar.

This book urges readers not to settle for mediocrity in the public arena but to strive for excellence. People in power must be held accountable for their actions. People of faith have an additional challenge: to be true to our religious beliefs and teachings.

Radicals hear a call to develop innovative interventions to foster justice. The biblical prophets demonstrate that imagination and creativity drive home God's message with power. According to the biblical climate, care and confrontation are the keys to strengthen congregations and communities. Religious leaders form interfaith partnerships, and diverse communities collaborate to restore life. Such a task is radical!

I use the term "radical" to mean one who practices nonviolent tactics to bring about social justice. And I consider myself to be a radical. Students of the Bible will quickly notice many of the techniques and strategies offered in this book mirror those practiced by Jesus Christ as portrayed in the Gospel According to Mark.[3] Radicals organize communities to engage in socially responsible actions to usher in sustainable changes to society. Radicals are not anti-power.

Radicals organize to build power to effect positive changes in communities and regions. Radicals are against the misuse of power over others without accountability. Protectors of the status quo, meanwhile, demonize radicals. Invitations for transparency and accountability are offensive demands to non-radicals and people who hold a different understanding of a democratic society. People with power to impact the social determinants of health without any accountability to the communities and demographics they affect are constantly attacking radicals in an attempt to quiet our voices and actions. The attacks range from hostile labels, ridicule, to character assassination and disinformation, violence, arrests, threats, fake news, and voter suppression. Radicals believe society can be democratic and just—that it is possible for all people to fully participate in the conversation about how communities are sustained and the planet is honored. Radicals can see hope where others see scapegoats, exploitation, profit, decay, and abandonment.

This book offers hope through stories of active, nonviolent community engagement. This book is filled with my reflections after decades of experience as an urban pastor, psychoanalyst, professor, and public advocate. There is a great cloud of witnesses and many mentors who formed my understanding of life as a radical. Each one added significantly to my education on the topic. *New Rules for Radicals: TNT for Faith-Based Leaders* represents what I learned from their mentorship and the painful yet informative lessons of firsthand experience.

Radicals embrace community organizing. Some people call the work community engagement. The big question this book examines is how people of faith cooperate to bring about justice and fairness through peaceful disruption and social change.

Let us start with four basic questions:

1. What is going on? Gather accurate information to separate fact from fiction.

xii New Rules for Radicals

2. Why is this reality going on? Interpret the root cause of actions through research and analysis.
3. What ought to be going on? Explore the options that ethical behavior dictates.
4. How might we respond? Strategize pragmatic action steps that align with the values, beliefs, and practices of people of faith.

These are the questions embedded in practical theology.[4] Seminary students learn that biblical prophets and contemporary faith-based leaders with a social justice mindset ask such questions. Today, souls who ask these questions tend to be labeled as radicals. Christian faith informs us radicals that our God-given duty is to point out evil and injustice with laser-like precision.

Read Scripture. Story after story documents that change is obtained through social disruption, confrontation, and negotiation. Like the prophets of the Bible, the Christian is attuned by God to see visions and hear sounds that elude others. Ours is a call to speak out and stand out! This behavior is considered radical. But it is a part of God's story (Deuteronomy 16:18-20). Our interfaith colleagues will attest that their sacred scriptures place expectations upon them to seek justice and fairness. Said differently, radicals are to help those in need and use our gifts (charisma) to secure justice (Micah 6:8).

Radicals are heavily armed with admittedly abrasive attitudes at times. People who carry the label "radical" can make mountains out of what others deem as molehills or commonplace. Moses is one such biblical example. "As soon as he came near the camp and saw the calf and the dancing, Moses' anger burned hot, and he threw the tablets from his hands and broke them at the foot of the mountain. He took the calf that they had made, burned it with fire, ground it to powder, scattered it on the water, and made the Israelites drink it" (Exodus 32:19-20, NRSV). Those of us in the Christian faith have Jesus as an example of the abrasive attitude and righteous anger of a faith leader. "Then Jesus entered the temple and drove out all who were selling and buying in the temple, and he overturned the tables of the money changers and the seats of those who sold doves. He said to them, 'It is written, "My house shall be called a house of prayer"; but you are making it a den of robbers'" (Matthew 21:12-13, NRSV). The unusually sharp vision and drastic behavior become a part of radicals' DNA.

All of us are aware that rampant violence, injustice, and evil exist. However, to the radical, no act of violence, harm, or injustice is insignificant. Radicals detest violence. In a world where apathy and complacency are rewarded and encouraged, being a compassionate advocate for others is radical. Our world needs radicals. Such souls provide hope.

Once you are fully clothed as a radical, you are calibrated to address even the slightest hint of evil without any fear of retribution. We radicals are social scientists who passionately proclaim dismay at injustice and challenge the status quo. God grants us great courage. This mindset becomes part of our DNA. The world needs new radicals.

Faith-based radicals never shrink from where evil takes place or from those who commit an evil deed. Be it presidents, potentates, politicians, pew personnel, poor people, preachers, or even popes, we are compelled to shine a light on that which is wrong. Our quandary is the ongoing tension between addressing communal decay in our social environment and the socially acceptable role of offering personal insights on individual spiritual health and growth. By nature, and job description, radicals must declare justice will not tolerate evil. It is a grueling task. Churches and communities need new radicals armed with the stories that matter.

xiv   New Rules for Radicals

# For Such a Time as This

Roberta Samet was the portfolio supervisor for the September 11th Fund's Care for the Caregivers Interfaith Project, which was funded by the New York Community Trust, the American Red Cross, and the United Way of New York City. She made it clear: any grantee of the September 11th Fund must complete a two-and-a-half-day workshop called "Undoing Racism." "And, Dr. Ashley, that includes you as the project director," Roberta uttered to me with a smile. "She is kidding, right?" I thought. "Maybe she missed that I am the Black guy in the room. I know a thing or two about racism." Roberta responded to my unspoken words, "Dr. Ashley, glance at the available dates for the workshops held by The People's Institute for Survival and Beyond.[5] Find the workshop date that fits your schedule. Sign up." I showed up for the workshop with an attitude: "Why am I here? Impress me." How the three trainers handled such an explosive topic amazed me. Their analysis of racism changed my life. What a difference a day makes.

Fast-forward eighteen years, and I have attended the workshop twenty times or more. Each time my attention picks up something I missed, or I hear the information differently. In America's racially charged climate, one needs a critical analysis of racism. It is important to understand historically, ideologically, and socially why we are a country divided by race.

One of the People's Institute's core trainers is Barbara Major, an energetic, sharp, tell-it-like-it-is Black woman who calls New Orleans home. President George W. Bush asked her to assume a leadership role in the rebuilding of New Orleans following Hurricane Katrina. She chaired the "Bring Back New Orleans Commission." Barbara is respected internationally for her groundbreaking work as the administrator of the St. Thomas Community Health Center,[6] which is located in one of the largest public housing complexes in the United

States. She also co-led the workshop at the New Brunswick Theological Seminary, the oldest Protestant seminary in North America.

During an "Undoing Racism" training session, Barbara strongly encouraged me to author this book. Barbara holds back no punches in the "Undoing Racism" workshops. In one of our many conversations, she said, "Will, you have to be clear about this stuff. Call it for what it is. You must author a book. That is your calling."

In addition to Barbara Major, other voices pushed me to write *New Rules for Radicals: TNT for Faith-Based Leaders*. College-age young adults asked for a resource for effective social action. (I remember being filled with hope at their tender age.) When I mentioned Saul Alinsky, the blank looks on their faces took me aback. They had not read his book, *Rules for Radicals*.[7] I wondered silently if these millennials were exposed to his brand of community engagement. Is it possible they did not know the contemporary roots of civic engagement? This experience was not an isolated case. I conducted conversations with hundreds of well-meaning citizens, each one in his or her own way out to make a difference in the world. The name Saul Alinsky did not ring a bell. I asked about the "Undoing Racism" workshop and received a similar blank look.

There was another audience who inspired me to author this book. They are the victims of an unjust society. These are hardworking, decent citizens who want their piece of the American dream. Power brokers reduce such people to pawns in a high-stakes chess game. Listening to their stories of pain and frustration pushed me to author a book that offers inspiration, information, and hope. People in targeted zip codes are dehumanized, demoralized, marginalized, monetized, and criminalized. *New Rules for Radicals: TNT for Faith-Based Leaders* is written to show there is hope when intergenerational, cross-cultural, interfaith communities work together.

I also wanted to revisit Alinsky's work. Radicals must address blatant racism, racial disparities, and white supremacy. Those are the elephants in the room. The unchecked radicalization of white supremacists has gone on too long without the church or society calling them out for their violent behavior and actions. On June 17, 2015, twenty-one-year-old Dylann Roof was welcomed into Bible study at the Emanuel African Methodist Episcopal Church in Charleston, South Carolina. Following Bible study and a prayer meeting, Roof, a young white supremacist, did the unthinkable. He opened fire in the church, killing nine Black parishioners. Unfortunately, this was not the first time radicalized white supremacists committed a violent act against Black people in a house of worship. Four Black little girls were killed in the bombing of the 16th Street Baptist Church in Birmingham, Alabama, on September 15, 1963. It took over a decade for the first conviction of this crime. Multiple decades passed before the others responsible for the bombing were brought to justice. Hope cannot be embraced without any attention to how racialized violence robs everybody of their humanity. These were the building blocks that led to authoring this book.

For all the reasons I already mentioned, authoring this book was a must for me. Seeing the world as I do through the lenses of a psychoanalyst, pastor, professor, and human, realities offered ample reasons to put pen to paper. Then, the world was hit with the coronavirus pandemic, unlike any in recent history, and it became clear that life as we knew it would never be the same. Saddened and angered by leadership voids, petty politics, and the thousands of lives lost, I found it became mandatory I write *New Rules for Radicals: TNT for Faith-Based Leaders*.

**Jeffrey Haggray**, executive director of American Baptist Home Mission Societies and Judson Press, concluded that COVID-19 spotlighted the experiences of vulnerable populations. For Jeffrey, this pandemic is "our national homework assignment," in which we must begin "to envision a just and inclusive society."[8] His perception of the challenges posed by the COVID-19 pandemic mirrors mine, which will be evident throughout the book. History has documented that paradigm shifts are expected following pandemics and large-scale disasters. Any sense of normalcy and stability is broken. New power dynamics among the elite emerge. What is presented and accepted as normal is renegotiated.

New realities result in the tremendous willingness of citizens to engage in conversations and actions that foster a sense of security and trust. People become obsessed, and rightfully so, with whether their needs will be met by the government, business, medicine, and the systems that drive economies. These are not new concerns. Such concerns are cut across geography and demographics. Understanding how oppression and hope operate in other countries was helpful in addressing such issues in the United States. The global health crisis and corresponding worldwide economic crisis demand something bold in response. Apathy and complacency are no longer acceptable. Citizens miraculously realize we can ill afford to watch politicians divide up the world passively. Our task becomes apparent. Together, we must save our world from those with agendas and practices that rob us of our dignity and humanity. Therein is our hope.

## Stories Have Power

People remember stories. Good stories grab our attention. Ask any bestselling novelist or successful television director. Hollywood banks on our love for stories; media moguls are in business to share stories. Orators infuse stories with life, speechwriters craft stories as their secret weapon, and politicians work at becoming storytellers. Read sacred literature or watch someone deliver a TED Talk. What captures the audience's attention and makes the speaker's points come alive are the stories. Stories become ingrained in our brains and we cannot get enough. Radicals collect and retell stories. The design of this book is to help you craft your story to bring hope to your community.

Imagine how humbled I was when God reminded me of the value of stories while I was in an assembly hall full of atheists and humanists and an ethical leader declared, "We do not have a theology." The statement challenged my Christian seminary education that required a theology to undergird moral actions. I reflected, "God, did you forget I'm a Black Baptist pastor, psychoanalyst, and professor? I make a living listening to stories and sharing stories from multiple sources." God made an excellent point, albeit in a strange place from the perspective of this card-carrying Christian; stories transcend lines of division, debate, and denominational pride. Booming out of the same assembly hall were the words that became the focus of this book: "What are the stories that will unite people of goodwill to take action? What stories offer hope?" In other words, what stories will equip people to engage in practical actions that bring about positive changes for the masses and contribute to the debate about humanity's future?

This is a global conversation and challenge, but I am ever mindful that all politics is local. My personal invitation is for you to join the discussion, equipped with new tools and an affirmation that your voice matters. Let your stories lead you to act. Your experiences matter! If this book is the catalyst for such activism, then my mission is accomplished!

This book is not intended to disparage the left or the right. The stories in this book speak to people of goodwill regardless of party affiliation or political leaning. I will talk politics, yet I will be mindful that both sides of the aisle are a part of the debate about humanity's future. Let us agree together to look with unbiased eyes at the challenges that face humanity. Various political parties and leaders of all stripes (local, regional, national, and global) share responsibility for the problems that make this conversation about the future of humanity more urgent. Radicals are needed to break the cycle of shame, blame, and games seasoned with more of the same once the next group gains power. Being a radical is different from being a zealot who is prone to violence if they do not get their way. Radicals play by a set of rules guided by sound spiritual practices that honor creation and the humanity in each and every person.

## Radicals Are Better Storytellers

"Rev. Ashley, you are radical!" said the reporter. Given my history, blessed with many years of living proud, a lifetime of advocacy work with marginalized and exploited communities, and swimming against the tide on controversial issues, I have been called far worse. Even so, shock registered on my face to hear those words from a middle-aged, local newspaper writer. "Sir, repeat yourself. What did you say?" I asked. The reporter looked me straight in the face and said with a smirk, "You are radical! Dr. Ashley, 'raving, ranting, radical' is what our elected officials, their staff, and key business leaders call you. What is your response?" After thirty-plus years serving as a senior pastor of four different Black congregations, teaching graduate courses as a tenured seminary professor, and seeing patients as a certified psychoanalyst, I knew I would not be well served by my normal tendencies to preach, teach, or analyze when responding to this reporter. Instead, I immediately thought, given my life's journey, to be called a radical is a badge of honor. I accepted the label and embraced it with pride. My deceased mother and father would be proud of their only son. I can envision the conversation. "Hey, Mom and Dad, a reporter called me a radical." My dad would respond, "What was the bad part?" Mom on the other hand, like so many Black and Latinx mothers, would register a look of worry on her face. "Son, be careful. Please do not give crazy, angry white supremacists any more reasons to target you."

In Harlem in the 1960s and 1970s, such a title and distinction was not a terrible thing. We wore the label radical with pride. Back then, radical meant unpredictable, fearless, scary, anti-establishment, risk-taking, advocating for the people, unafraid to meet violence with violence, and generally crazy. The '60s and '70s were the flower child era. Peace, pot, and the pill were the order of the day. "I'm okay, you're okay, it's okay" was a common expression. However, being counted as a radical was a double-edged sword. In the eyes of the challenged masses, you were a hero, a champion for justice, and a voice for the voiceless. On the other hand, from the perspective of the keepers of the status quo, you were a threat to be neutralized or eliminated. History and declassified documents detail the many law enforcement and governmental agencies, such as the Federal Bureau of Investigation[9] and the Central Intelligence Agency,[10] that designed programs with the sole goal of dismantling any forms of resistance, efforts to end racism, sexism, and police abuse, or challenges to the distribution of wealth. Is this idea what the reporter was trying to tease out of me? How does one answer a journalist who is out to get a story and, in so doing, is willing to make you the story? Should caution be the order of the day? I reminded myself, "Willard, there is an agenda behind the reporter's statement and inquiry. Remember, do not personalize this conversation. Keep the focus on your concerns for the community. Be repetitive in your expressions of empathy for people in pain. Seize the moment! Rev. Ashley, you are a radical. Own it with pride!"

Understandably, radical can be a scary word. Patients shudder when a physician uses that term for planned surgery or diagnosis. Anxiety and fear are typical reactions if a person hears they need a radical prostatectomy or radical mastectomy. Socially, the term suggests someone who zealously takes a stance outside of traditional and socially acceptable thinking. Baby boomers will tell you Generation X and millennials are "radically different" than their own generation. Technology and failed attempts to make a lasting difference in the world ensured that the younger generations would appear radical compared to older generations. Organized teenagers who protest policies and practices are not new. Look at the Civil Rights movement. It was led by women who never received the credit due them,[11] college students, teenagers, clergy of various faiths, and people of goodwill. What is new and radical is the use of social media to organize, publicize, and tell one's story. It is a progressive game changer.

Politically, the word radical is used to shut down and label a person with an opposing view who challenges status quo thinking. He or she may even be accused of antisocial behavior or prone to violence. Politicians usually describe a person as a radical to quiet their voice, dilute any amassed power, and chase away would-be followers. Martin Luther King Jr. was called a radical. Perhaps applying the term to Malcolm X or Black Lives Matter better makes the point. The playbook to discredit radicals is universal. Tools of the trade are to reframe or mischaracterize the radical's stated mission; fail to acknowledge or publicize the person's positive accomplishments; lie about the individual's or group's perceived threat to society; demonize the radical's cause so that people of goodwill walk away; and attack their leadership. (More on this in later chapters.)

The word radical is also applied to persons who practice their religion or rituals in ways that are foreign to others' thinking and cause discomfort. Being Muslim does not automatically make a person a radical, even though some politicians and groups would have people think that is the case.[12]

We in the United States are taught to fear and demonize "the other," the people and groups we do not know or do not understand.

I knew clearly what was at stake when that reporter asked me how I responded to being called a radical. He echoed the sentiments of people who had an ax to grind about my accomplishments in the community and who attempted to cause those who supported my ministry to distance themselves from me. For them, calling me a radical was a technique to minimize the community demands as unreasonable or to portray me as an insane person, at worst, or at best someone who did not understand how the political system works. The community and its leaders should be patient, my detractors said; change does not happen overnight.

When such labels work, it puts clergy back in the box. You know the one: preach on the weekends, visit the sick, pray, sing, conduct your holy rituals, do not involve yourself with issues of justice, stay in your lane. This view holds clergy should stay out of anything with political overtones, the exception being appearing with politicians who welcome our voice and influence to support their candidacy at election time. The unwritten rules of the box are that clergy are to dispense spiritual valium to keep the masses calm, not ask questions, run away from any accurate analysis that calls for fairness or suggests a policy was in the best interest of business or politicians rather than the people, and absolutely not upset the one percent who own most wealth and the means of production.

Years of experience taught me that a politician, who does not like the tone of a story, can call the publisher or owner of the channel who will see that the story is dead or watered down to remove the bite. Ministers are expected to play nice with the people who influence elected officials at all levels. We are expected not to disturb the global power brokers who trade zillions of dollars in a real live Monopoly game. Yes, Rev. Ashley from Harlem, the son of southern parents, is a radical.

Words have power. Words can build up or destroy. The creative use of words can define a person and redefine their causes. Another reason for authoring this book is that good-hearted people who organize for justice are often naïve to the tricks played by politicians, power brokers, and puppet masters who control policies and practices behind the scenes. These tricksters are smart enough to hire people who reword well-meaning intentions and demonize radicals' work using labels and emotionally charged imagery. These are the same power players who attempt to identify your spokespersons for you—usually, someone in their pocket who is oriented to acceptable behavior or someone who at least will not cause waves. Knowing all of this, I wondered what really led that reporter to ask me to respond to being called a radical. Here was an opportunity to educate the reporter, if no one else.

The reporter, anxiously awaiting my answer with pad and pen in hand, exhibited a look that said, "Answer the question." With a devilish grin on my face and slowly paced speech as if to say, "I will give you time to write down my answer accurately," I started to respond to the reporter. "Yes, I am a radical. My theological beliefs, biblical interpretation, understanding of humanity, worldviews, values, and personality leave me with no other choice. It's in my DNA. Call me radical. I call it Christian and what God expects of religious leaders. Jesus was a radical. He staged public theatre to bring home a point. Jesus was an excellent storyteller. Jesus appreciated the need to be responsible for human beings, good citizens with a spiritual core that treats all of God's creation with dignity and respect. He was not an isolationist or a Lone Ranger. Jesus understood the value of multiple communities working together in collaboration. Jesus understood that no one person can change the world alone. Sir, to be a radical, in my usage of the word, is to be like Jesus." The reporter appeared uncertain what to do with my response. He put his head down and wrote. The professor and preacher in me continued.

"Radicals have rules. Radicals work with a team of colleagues who conduct extensive research on an issue before we act. We ask people what is important in their lives and what they want to change in their neighborhood. We listen! Our leaders ask people about their dreams, fears, and hopes. We are intentional about being ethical in our behavior, yet not afraid to be unpredictable. We identify leaders in the community and offer training to enhance their skills. Like good debate team members or lawyers, we look at an issue from all sides. We analyze who has the power to do what and we examine their self-interests. Our leaders wrestle with the impact of racism, sexism, and classism and include the reality of such in our research. Our training pushes us to examine definitions and word usage closely. We explore what each player in this drama exactly will receive if he or she gets their way. We are careful to follow the money, and we ask how economic considerations drive the issue.

"Our team conducts an honest evaluation of what is at stake for each person, from decision-makers, to influence-peddlers, to the masses seeking justice. Our team takes a realistic view of what is a win. We eat together, pray for one another, and share in each other's lives. We care for each other. In so doing, we exchange healthy habits. Shared wisdom helps us with time management, self-care, and unique clergy stresses. We support each other as we learn how to be effective in our ministries. Our leaders struggle with each other and our congregations on the tough questions with no easy answers.

"Together we design a strategy to stand before the decision-makers to voice our perspectives. Radicals rehearse before an action. We know there are no quick fixes, and the fight may be a rollercoaster ride with ups and downs along the way. Thus, we pray together. Reading groups are formed to share books and reflect on the victories and struggles of other leaders. Armed with all this information and inspiration, we tell a story. It's our stories that win the day. Radicals are remarkable storytellers! We tell better stories. Thus, my short answer is I am a radical."

My conversation with this reporter never made it to print. My responses were buried. Nevertheless, I know it was educational for the reporter. Later feedback from others was the reporter shared my response as a cheat sheet and blueprint for persons who want to get inside the mindset of radicals. *New Rules for Radicals: TNT for Faith-Based Leaders* is an expansion, exposition, and embodiment of my dialogue with the reporter.

This book is designed to help you better tell your story to committees, congregations, communities, and collectives who possess the power to bring about positive change. Telling good stories is the secret weapon that is not so secret. It is the pitch the batter sees coming but cannot hit. It is playing basketball against my son; my brain knows what he is going to do next, but my banged-up, aging body says, "Lots of luck if you depend on me to slide your feet to stop him."

Radicals are better storytellers. We enlist raw emotions. We get people to stop and think. Our stories cannot be ignored. With our stories, we unite, polarize, and comfort. We offer hope. Any relevant story pushes the listener to ask, "How can I help?" Jewish rabbis and Black preachers tend to be excellent storytellers. Their stories paint vivid pictures. When we listen to their stories, we can identify with the characters. The story draws us in and makes us realize that character could be, or is, me. In stories we hear pain, laughter, pastoral concern, defeat, victory, and encouragement. One of the many goals of this book is to help you, reader and fellow radical, paint informative, inspirational, insightful pictures that tell a story so you can secure results for your cause. Radicals are better storytellers.

## You Are a Radical!

You have the book. Thank you! Maybe the title caught your attention. Perhaps some professor chose the book as required reading for a course, or your friends or colleagues picked this text for your book club selection. It could be that curiosity got the best of you, so you are reading the book. You may be one of those souls who grew up on Saul Alinsky's community organizing principles and, like me, you want to know what has changed in the years since his book *Rules for Radicals*. Or maybe the premise of my book—congregations collaborating to bring about changes in the community—excites you. People of goodwill usually come alive at the opportunity to bring about positive outcomes when dealing with issues of concern.

Let us build on our earlier transparency and honesty. The word "radical" may have you a little on edge. There is something inside of us that quietly struggles at times with being considered a radical. Admittedly, the word comes with historical baggage and modern-day demonization. Many people tend to think of radicals as zealous extremists who take to violence. On the milder side, radicals are painted as social misfits who make unreasonable demands or who missed the memo that this is not the era of the 1970s flower child.

I vividly remember the first time someone called me a radical. The term secretly frightened me. Did it mean I was not a good citizen? Was this an indictment on my character or a call to unearth a clinical diagnosis to work out in therapy? How would my family, friends, and congregation react to hearing or reading my name attached to such a word? Given all the world's violence, is it safe to be a radical or to be labeled a radical? Being called a radical or calling another person by that term receives reactions.

This word may not be the one you use to describe yourself.

However, once you seek change, "radical" may be the name assigned to you. Once "no" is not an acceptable answer and you decide to act, all your relationships change and so does your name. This reality will be evident in the chapters that follow. Know that in back rooms, some clever people spin the truth to make it difficult to discern fact from fiction. Such souls see any threat to the status quo or their agenda as radical.

Some will be quick to label this book the work of a crazy conspiracy theorist. The glaringly guilty may try other strategies to dismiss the truths in this book. This book results from a lifetime of firsthand experiences working to bring about justice, foster social change, and serve communities that have been demonized, marginalized, monetized, criticized, scandalized, and stigmatized. As I tell seminarians and seasoned clergy, once you collaborate to change systems that rob persons of their dignity, to question the distribution of wealth, and to fight for outcomes that really upgrade the quality of life for the masses, you become a target. Most people do not want to believe institutions and those in power will work doubly hard to keep things as they are with only window dressing changes.[13] We want to believe our elected officials, institutions, and systems are all working for our good. There are some awesome women and men who do work tirelessly on behalf of their districts, regions, and countries and such souls should be applauded and appreciated. However, this tireless generosity is not universal. It takes money to run a political campaign, and too often that money comes with strings, lobbyists, and paybacks. Look at what committees your state and federally elected legislators seat on. Then for fun, research what action groups, lawyers, accountants, financial institutions, and Fortune 100 companies donated to their election efforts.[14] It is little wonder why some decision-makers resist efforts to ensure significant policies, laws, and practices to improve the social determinates of life for the masses. Radicals' compassion for others leads to our call to fight for a better community, work for justice, and change the world. This book offers a process and practical tools to help you achieve your desire for a better world.

Friend, a word of caution. Once you want to challenge the status quo, you are playing hardball with players who throw one-hundred-mile-per-hour fastballs at your head in hopes you are hit and injured.[15] Nevertheless, remember, we have a spiritual core to keep us grounded, encouraged, supported, loved, and courageous. You do this! Yes, you are a radical.

## The Making of a Radical

Radicals are like biblical prophets. What seems like a minor injustice to some people is a significant offense to a radical. Saul Alinsky was a radical. In his biography Alinsky embraces the term rebel.[16] His focus was on the Have-Nots. His question was, "Can people without clear paths of influence seize the power necessary for their voices to be heard, valued, and respected to the point decisions are made to benefit the masses instead of in the interests of the elite?" For taking on such a task with remarkable success, some gave him credit for being the father of modern-day organizing. Alinsky's appeal was mostly to the white middle-class.[17] He did have an influence on Latinx and Black leaders. However, leaders of minority communities were organizing long before Alinsky. We think our very survival was, is, and will continue to be how we effectively organize communities. Our realities and organizing experiences predate Saul Alinsky, and the principles learned from them have informed many revolts, movements, and campaigns of active organizers since the beginning of humanity. Ask any preacher who serves a congregation with a constitution in place that allows for pastors to be voted in or out. Mentors cautioned us as young pastors that if you do not keep a careful eye on the organizers in your congregation, your complainers will organize you right out of your pulpit. During the midpoint of my career, I was reminded of that hard lesson firsthand. Clergy share horror stories and work while wounded because of battles fought against organized naysayers in the congregation.

Founded in 1940, the Industrial Areas Foundation (IAF)[18] continues the work of Saul Alinsky. I have benefited dramatically over a couple of decades from their workshops, wisdom, critical analysis, strategies, books, support, encouragement, and friendships. Parts of this book could not have been written without the guidance and learnings from IAF leaders, organizers, and friends. My leadership skills and profile grew because of working with the IAF. Their model of inclusion spoke to my spirit. Those of us working with the IAF learned not to allow our differences to divide us. We found victory working together to bring about positive changes for our communities: Jewish, Muslim, Catholic, Unitarian, Humanist, Protestant, Hindu, straight, gay, queer, lesbian, Democrats, Republicans, political insiders, academics, philanthropists, and the socially conscious rich.

Other active organizations supply comparable training and use similar principles. The IAF way is not the only way to organize. But I am partial to the IAF. We have shared some incredible moments and impossible victories. Michael Gecan, former co-director for the IAF, is a contributor to my second book; his chapter is entitled "The Universal Tools of Effective Leadership."[19] Michael regularly writes editorial opinions and offers critical analysis on the day's hot political news topics, and he encourages community and religious leaders to do the same. This practice is another way to have your voice heard through the power of the media. We will visit this tactic in greater detail later in this book.

If you have not attended an IAF training, I strongly suggest that you do so sooner than later. Yes, even if you are a seasoned organizer, there is value in sitting in an IAF workshop. Hopefully, the stories and strategies from this book will move you to invest in learning more about how to organize, be heard, and engage in smart self-care. Many of the stories in this book were born out of IAF experiences and encounters. Saul Alinsky may or may not have been the father of modern organizing. He did, however, move the discipline forward and gave many of us succinct, successful, and enjoyable tools to combat being invisible, ignored, and impotent. He was a social worker, not a pastor, imam, priest, rabbi, or spiritual leader.

My perspectives will vary from Alinsky's given my experience as a pastor who is accountable to a congregation and their leadership. Besides, I show up in the world as a 6'2", light-skinned, Black man in America. However, please read Alinsky's book and his successors' works, specifically Ed Chambers and Michael Gecan. Such reading is insightful and provides a bridge to appreciate that my writing is a continuation of the work of Saul Alinsky. One may argue that much has happened since Alinsky published his seminal book in 1971 and, in some ways, nothing has changed. My book aims to speak to both realities.

## Race Matters

If there is a critique of Alinsky and the IAF, their handling of race and racism leaves an army of people of color disappointed. Recent efforts to address this concern are applauded. Meanwhile, numerous voices and visionaries have spoken to the reality that race matters. Quite often, it is the elephant in the room that few, if any, want to discuss. It lacks integrity to write about congregations, collaboration, and community change without being honest about the impact of racism in America and worldwide. Many colleagues have written more eloquently about this topic than I do in this book. I strongly suggest you read past and present literature on the role of religion in racism. Look at US history in forming policies and laws that disadvantage people of color, especially Black souls. Sadly, the church universal has often been on the wrong side of this struggle. History reveals complicity with white supremacy and the outright blessing of racist concepts and practices.[20] Lynchings took place right after church on Sundays, as gruesome pictures show.

As stated earlier, The People's Institute for Survival and Beyond offers a workshop entitled "Undoing Racism."[21] The focus of their work is teaching leaders how to organize. The dynamics of race and racism offer a context. The "Undoing Racism" workshop principles serve as the foundation to teach participants how to reclaim our common humanity.

Founded by two Black men, The People's Institute trainers and organizers travel worldwide to conduct this workshop. The workshop provides a unique analysis of racism in America and defines racism in a way that casts a much wider net of what it means to be a racist. Religious leaders in the New York City metro area are working with the co-founder, Ron Chisom; interim director, Kimberly Richards; Joseph Barndt, Shadia Alvarez, Imani Chapman, Nathan Trice; and other faith-based organizers aligned with The People's Institute. Our goal is to develop a model for spiritual, ethical, and religious leaders to identify and dismantle racism within their communities, congregations, and denominations and within the larger society. Radicals are governed by a set of principles, or rules, if you will. These rules include dismantling racism.

Racism impacts the social determinates of the quality of life. Racists attempt to escape responsibility for racism by scapegoating people of color, being ignorant of history, and disputing the information. There are good examples of how words matter, as does who has the power to define terms. Racists attempt to escape responsibility for the problem by underscoring how Black people express years of anger, frustration, and abuse. By how I show up in the world, illustrations of the role of race and racism are embedded in these stories.

## Four Personal Stories

Four watershed firsthand experiences inform and inspire this book. First, as noted earlier, I designed and directed the largest clergy resiliency project in the United States following the tragic events of September 11, 2001. Seven thousand interfaith spiritual caregivers in the five boroughs of New York City found healing and help through a five-year project entitled, "The Care for the Caregivers Interfaith Project: A Ministry of the Council of Churches of the City of New York (CCCNY)." The project was funded by the New York Community Trust who gave oversight to the September 11th Fund, The United Way, and the American Red Cross. The Rockefeller Foundation was responsible for the project's financial control to ensure our accounting practices could withstand the scrutiny of the New York media and were above reproach.

The task was not simple: organize the spiritual leaders in the largest city in the country; assess their mental health; provide tools so those religious leaders can assess the mental health of their flock; be a bridge between the clergy and mental health professionals; and finally, offer culturally humble tools for self-care. In doing this work, the portfolio supervisor for several projects funded by the September 11th Fund, Roberta Samet, was my advocate and became a lifelong friend. She helped me navigate the political waters of New York City and encouraged my creativity. When CCCNY was authorized to receive the first grant, Roberta insisted that I run the project or no funds would be distributed, to the dismay of some. Some of the religious leaders left our project and formed their own response network. However unintentional it may have been, that revealed the religious politics in the big city and the appearance of racism. Throughout the book, you find references to the lessons learned about organizing communities because of this project.

The second experience is still active and long-term. In the spring of 1986, I resigned as the director of recruitment and assistant dean of students at Andover Newton Theological School to take on the position of senior pastor of the historic Monumental Baptist Church, Jersey City, New Jersey. The church boasted of 1,500 members on the rolls. Three hundred offering envelopes were counted every Sunday. When I resigned in 1996, the church had 2,500 members and three Sunday worship services. I followed a beloved pastor who had served the congregation for forty-two years, and his predecessor had served Monumental for forty years. The experience of coming behind long-term leaders is a book for another day. Monumental was a pillar in the local Black community and beyond. Every Black History Month, on the second Sunday in February, the congregation distributed $40,000 between eight different not-for-profits. The Who's Who of the Black community attended Monumental Baptist Church.

Early on, I was approached by Father Kenneth Letoile, a Catholic priest, about joining an interfaith clergy group focused on community activism and social change. Such a critical congregation as Monumental needed to be part of this new effort. The group was being trained and supervised by the Industrial Areas Foundation (IAF). We formed an organization in Hudson County, New Jersey, and called ourselves the Interfaith Community Organization (ICO). We racked up several victories, both small and large. Historians and a few reporters suggested we were vital in sending some corrupt politicians to serve time in country club-like prisons.

ICO decided to address the affordable housing crisis in Jersey City. Our goal was to build two hundred owner-occupied affordable homes within walking distance of Monumental Baptist Church. "Will, how hard can it be?" I will never forget six words from Father Geoff Curtiss, rector of All Saints Episcopal Parish in Hoboken, New Jersey. Years later, in retelling the story to New Jersey Governor Phil Murphy at a meeting in his office, Governor Murphy replied with a smile, "And you found out it is very hard." It has taken ICO more than thirty years, multiple governors, numerous mayors, countless trips to the Department of Environmental Protection (DEP), and a federal class-action lawsuit to make any progress, plus turning down $50 million to walk away and constant threats to our well-being, not to mention media attacks. Geoff and I laugh at his question thirty-plus years later. We organized money and people to push the local politicians to build affordable housing. We did not know the property was toxic. Nor did we fully appreciate at first that something as seemingly simple as trying to build affordable housing could put us on the radar of the president of the United States Bill Clinton. In going after polluters, we unknowingly attacked a close friend of the president. I am a Black Baptist preacher. We are prone to narcissistic tendencies, and these become even more pronounced when you have your weekly television program on Black Entertainment Television (BET) in your mid-thirties. Healthy ego aside, I never expected to garner such attention in high places. You will read much more about this thirty-plus-year fight in later chapters.

Third, COVID-19 changed all the rules of social interaction. The coronavirus pandemic exposed all the reasons radicals are needed in society. Daily headlines confronted readers with disparities in health care and bickering among political parties. At the same time, thousands died, necessary resources became impossible to secure, half-baked strategies that did nothing more than line the pockets of political allies were implemented, and a total lack of compassion in favor of saving the economy to keep one's power took hold. This global tragedy was a wake-up call for the complacent masses, who were given a front-row seat to the ugly side of politics and power.

Record unemployment and mass deaths grabbed the public's attention and stirred a desire for societal change. The pandemic also taught a new wave of radicals how to use technology and software applications to organize creatively and effectively. Any book that picks up where Saul Alinsky left off must now add the lament and renewed hope found in the COVID-19 pandemic stories.

Fourth, this book was written because I conduct clergy webinars, retreats, and workshops following mass killings, natural disasters, drive-by shootings, violence, racial protests, and widespread unrest. One thing is clear: Caregivers, spiritual leaders, and community activists are overwhelmed by the demands placed on us and often over the long haul. Congregational leaders seem unappreciative of the sacrifice and commitment required to engage in social justice issues. How does one create a healthy balance? Along with this current reality is a growing army of well-intentioned people of goodwill who lack the training necessary to endure long-term fights for justice. My prayer is that *New Rules for Radicals: TNT for Faith-Based Leaders* offers hope to these realities.

## The Big Questions

We began this introduction with four basic questions. Allow me to end it with more questions. In academia, it is called the big question. It is the central question that seeks an answer. In this case, there are a few big questions to be answered in this book.

- What can we learn from biblical stories that informs, encourages, and supports activism?

- How can faith-based leaders collaborate to ensure sustainable positive outcomes in their communities?
- What innovative approaches are effective in organizing for change?
- What lessons can we learn about community engagement through Fortune 100 companies, United Nations non-governmental agencies, not-for-profits, and the new mass movements?

The next eight chapters address these questions. Use the book as a tool and a process to organize your communities. Think big picture, intersections, and systems. Take what you need to be successful in your context. Read each chapter with a view toward collaboration to challenge and change the status quo. May the stories and insights in this book help you to restore hope. We are in this fight together. You are in my prayers!

## NOTES

1. "Herstory," Black Lives Matter, https://blacklivesmatter.com/herstory/, accessed June 5, 2020.

2. AP, "Obama Responds to Civil Unrest Following George Floyd's Death," https://abc7chicago.com/barack-obama-town-hall-george-floyd/6229479/, accessed February 12, 2021.

3. Ched Myers, *Binding the Strong Man: A Political Reading of Mark's Story of Jesus* (Maryknoll, NY: Orbis Books, 2006).

4. Richard Osmer, *Practical Theology: An Introduction* (Grand Rapids, MI: William B. Eerdmans, 2008), location 91 of 3256 in Kindle.

5. The People's Institute for Survival and Beyond was founded by two Black men who felt most organizing efforts fell short in an analysis of racism and its impact on society. To learn more about the organization and its work, see its website: http://www.pisab.org.

6. To learn more about St. Thomas Community Health Center, see its website: https://www.stthomaschc.org.

7. Saul D. Alinsky, *Rules for Radicals: A Pragmatic Primer for Realistic Radicals* (New York: Vintage Books, 1971).

8. Jeffery Haggray, "Our National Homework Assignment—Beginning

to Envision a Just and Inclusive Society," *The Christian Citizen*, April 1, 2020, https://christiancitizen.us/our-national-homework-assignment-beginning-to-envision-a-just-and-inclusive-society/, accessed February 6, 2021.

9. Kenneth O'Reilly, "Racial Matters," *The FBI's Secret File on Black America*, 1960–1972 (New York: The Free Press, 1989).

10. Nick Tomich. "COINTELPRO and CHAOS: How the FBI and the CIA Suppressed Dissent in the 1960s," Medium, March 4, 2020, https://medium.com/history-of-yesterday/cointelpro-and-chaos-how-the-fbi-and-the-cia-suppressed-dissent-in-the-1960s-8edc4bf3b248, accessed February 12, 2021.

11. Danielle L. McGuire, *At the Dark End of the Street* (New York: Alfred A. Knopf, 2010).

12. Tamer Elnoury and Kevin Maurer, *American Radical: Inside the World of an Undercover Muslim FBI Agent* (New York: Penguin Random House, 2018), 16.

13. G. William Domhoff, *Who Rules America? The Triumph of the Corporate Rich*, 7th ed. (New York: McGraw-Hill Education, 2014), x–xi.

14. The Center for Public Integrity, *Citizen Muckraking: How to Investigate and Right Wrongs in Your Community* (Monroe, ME: Common Courage Media, 2000), Kindle edition.

15. This reference along with the previous ones related to violence toward radicals is to underscore the danger radicals face and highlight the extent power brokers will go to maintain the status quo. Karl Evanzz, *The Judas Factor: The Plot to Kill Malcolm X* (New York: Thunder Mouth's Press, 1992).

16. Sanford D. Horwitt, *Let Them Call Me Rebel: Saul Alinsky His Life and Legacy* (New York: Alfred A. Knopf, Inc., 1989), 167.

17. Howitt, 533.

18. See the Industrial Areas Foundation website for their history, global victories, affiliates, and workshops: http://www.industrialareasfoundation.org.

19. Willard W.C. Ashley Sr., ed., *Learning to Lead: Lessons in Leadership for People of Faith* (Woodstock, NY: Skylight Paths Publishing, 2013), 31–39.

20. Jemar Tisby, *The Color of Compromise: The Truth About the American Church's Complicity with Racism* (Grand Rapids, MI: Zondervan, 2019).

21. Read the People's Institute website for more information about their history, resources, workshops, and opportunities for collaboration. See https://www.pisab.org.

# CHAPTER 1

# CONTEXT: KNOW YOUR SETTING

## Context Makes a Difference!

Clergy and lay leaders who preach or teach understand the importance of context and take great pains to ensure that sermons and Bible studies include the context of the passage. The first task of a radical is to conduct an environmental scan. Your goal is to understand your setting entirely. Learning about your context is fun and exciting. Put on your detective hat. Start investigating.

The late Frederick G. Sampson, the esteemed pastor of the Tabernacle Missionary Baptist Church in Detroit, Michigan, explained context this way: "Put three men in a room. Watch them kick, punch, and hit each other with wooden objects; we call it violence. Put 'Three Stooges' in the caption; we call it a comedy." Context makes a difference.

Go back to April 29–May 4, 1992. These five days are referred to by some as the Rodney King riots. The dates mark an ugly moment in our United States history. Los Angeles was the scene of riots and civil disturbances that left fifty people dead, over two thousand people injured, one thousand buildings destroyed, and damages well over one billion dollars. According to CNN, more than 6,500 National Guard troops were dispatched to restore order.[1] The civil unrest and violence in Los Angeles were an outpouring of anger in Black communities over the acquittal of four white police officers who were caught on video beating an unarmed Black man named Rodney King. The evidence of a crime was crystal clear to all but the jury.

I remember like yesterday a phone call from James Florio, governor of New Jersey, and Bill Bradley, senator from New Jersey. They asked, "Reverend, do we need to walk together through the streets of Newark, Camden, and Jersey City?" My sobering response was, "We are good in New Jersey. We are angry, but we intend to express our outrage through the political process." I thought this ended my involvement in such an ugly slice of history.

It was not too long afterwards that the phone rang again. This time it was a mentor and dear friend, Wyatt Tee Walker. He was the senior pastor of the Canaan Baptist Church in Harlem, New York. You may recall Wyatt served as the chief of staff to Martin Luther King Jr. Thus, Wyatt knew about organizing mass movements and he often shared his trade secrets with me on the topic.

"Will, it's Wyatt on the phone. Is your passport in order? We need to board a plane to South Korea." After a few deep breaths and increasing curiosity, I responded, "Yes, Wyatt, my passport is up to date." This was not our first time flying overseas together. Wyatt had invited me to go with him and a blue-ribbon collection of internationally known Black pastors to visit the home of Nelson Mandela in South Africa within days of his release from prison. Mandela wanted to thank us personally for our support and to acknowledge the risks we took as clergy to shine a light on apartheid. Wyatt knew first-hand my comfort level with political protocol and my ease with speaking to dignitaries.

"Will, pack your bags!" Wyatt said. "The president of South Korea, the South Korean chamber of commerce, and the senior pastors of the largest congregations in South Korea have scheduled meetings with us. During the Rodney King riots, the Korean stores and businesses in Black neighborhoods were vandalized. They want to know why. We are going with a team of Black pastors, which includes E. K. Bailey and you. E. K. will be your roommate on the trip." What an honor on so many levels. Chief among the honors was to room with E. K. Bailey. He was nationally known for organizing a preaching conference in his name. I did not know until the trip to South Korea that E. K. was also gifted in telling jokes and keeping people laughing. For ten days straight, we had nationally respected Black preachers on the floor in tears as we told jokes, often about the events of the day. One joke was at the expense of our fearless leader, Wyatt Tee Walker. At two o'clock one morning there was a pounding on our hotel door, and someone shouted, "Wake up!" E. K. and I looked at each other. We knew the voice; it was Wyatt. "Get up." Being closest to the door, I stumbled over to open it. "Hi, fearless leader, what is the urgency?" I said with my most disingenuous voice. E. K. followed my lead, "Fearless leader, what is the matter? Why are you up?" Wyatt responded with a big smile, "I heard what you two said about me. You said I took sick yesterday and was bedridden because I preached at the largest church in the world, and instead of taking up an offering, the pastor gave me a check." We responded after we stopped laughing, "Guilty as charged."

Jokes aside, the big day arrived. We were cleared by security and, with student protesters across the street, ushered into a meeting room to await the arrival of the president of South Korea. If the red carpeted steps leading to the second floor were not breathtaking enough, the lavish trappings in the conference room where we were to meet overwhelmed us.

After a short wait, the president and his entourage entered the room. We stood and bowed. The president extended his hand for us to shake. We exchanged greetings with him and his entourage. We sat.

It is not unusual in Black culture to introduce yourself to strangers. If you have southern roots or an upbringing below the Mason-Dixon line, you say hello to everybody regardless of your politics, ethnicity, or racial preferences. Be it for reasons of anxiety, unaware of security measures beyond what one could see, or something only God knows, E. K. looked at the president of South Korea, smiled his trademark smile, and then innocently said, "Mr. President, you do not know me, but I am E. K. Bailey from Texas." There was a hush in the room. Wyatt looked at me, and I looked back at Wyatt. E. K., sitting to my left, looked at me with an expression like, "What did I say?" Finally, the president's press secretary said with a wide smile, "Dr. Bailey, you are sitting two feet away from our president, who invited you to this meeting. We know all about you, your work, fame, and good-hearted nature." After that, the press secretary looked at Wyatt Tee Walker to make his point and said, "Dr. Walker, the checks you wrote before you boarded the plane at JFK airport cleared." It was a lesson on context. Ninety-nine percent of the time, what E. K. did with his introduction was the right thing, and had he done anything less, our elders would have called him on it. However, in this meeting, our identity and any additional required information were known long before we stepped onto the plane in New York City. Context makes a difference!

Whether preaching a sermon, sitting in front of a head of state, or engaging with power brokers, context makes a difference. One size does not fit all. What worked in one setting may not work somewhere else. Context drives our choice of action. Context gives our theology a home. Before you engage in action, invest the time to learn and know your context.

## Radicals Understand the Context of Their Times

"The church is irrelevant." Community leaders, scholars, and scores of disgruntled former congregants have sung this chorus repeatedly. Young people who are actively trying to make this a better world have expressed no interest in organized religion. Pressed as to why their disinterest in the sacred institution, they usually respond with, "The church is totally out of touch with today." Comedians have openly joked that the church no longer answers the big questions. Church leaders have played it safe. The church has given in to mounting pressure to conform and to be careful not to make waves. Clergy have placed their focus on affirmation from politicians and influential leaders instead of standing on high moral ground. Critics of the church have rightly called religious leaders to account. People expect leaders to lead, to push the envelope to be out front and in front of issues that matter. Leaders take risks, knowing full well that risks come at a cost. Religious leaders are called to put our sacred texts into action. Such behavior is radical. It is a lived theology.

People are clamoring for leadership from the church. Professional athletes, celebrities, and politicians have filled the void left by a silent church. Riots, mass protests, marches, and multiple expressions of anger and discontent have replaced the voices of competent, respected church leaders. Where are the collective voices of the church on issues of police brutality, health disparities, criminalization, food deserts, unequal education, wealth gaps, and targeted violence? Who are the church leaders that strike fear and respect in the seats of power? Who are the church leaders that are respected, leading justice movements for the masses, and followed in the seats of power? Is fear a factor that church leaders must have to be a leader? Take your time. I will wait for your answer.

Our context may vary, but there are some universals. The church has been afraid to be radical or has been too compromised to be taken seriously. People are looking for Jesus in the Bible. You can keep the well-dressed, polished, timid cult leaders seen in pulpits on Sundays. Seminary professors in ethics train students that congregations and communities expect clergy to speak to the tenor of the times and lead the masses into action. Clergy, do your job! Each of us has a specific context. Radicals are expected to know and understand their context. God expects clergy to interpret for the masses what is going on and how we are going to tackle it.

Make no mistake, being radical takes on another dimension when you preach, teach, visit, lead, and are accountable to the same group of people each week. Diplomacy is necessary to maintain your base while speaking out. I get it! Seated in your pews are people from both sides of the political aisle or from what some call purple states. Various congregation members see the world and current events with a diverse set of eyes and ears. Radicals are not always met with adoration by the congregation. However, that is not permission to be silent and take the easy road on the big issues. From the perspective of a seasoned Black Baptist pastor, we are in this mess because clergy have been too afraid to speak truth to power. So, we await the next MLK to speak for us and lead us into the promise land.

Do your diligent research. Join the fight. Work with colleagues to bring about change. Line up your facts. Learn how to hit, when to hit, and where to hit. Act based on the research of your context. Be radical. Answer the challenge to put Scripture into action. Organize! Be ready to pay the cost for your discipleship. Keep studying your context. Learn from the COVID-19 pandemic. Remember the protests following the murder of George Floyd. Respect your context. Matters of race do not impact every citizen or geography in the same manner. Context matters. But do something. Act!

## Ministry Is about Relationships

Radicals major in relationships. Ministry is about relationships. Any study of context is an examination of the numerous networks of relationships. Radicals understand that scrutinizing context is an opportunity to learn how the various systems and institutions impact relationships. Faith-based leaders too often major in bureaucratic tasks (budgets, buildings, and bulletins) to the detriment of relationship. Context allows a look at the stories behind the relationships and networks.

The Black church held the belief for centuries that the only way to be Christian, Jewish, Islamic, or any other expression of faith is to be radical.[2] With this theological mandate, Black clergy have taken unpopular stands for justice even if the reactions to their protests resulted in violence, injury, hardship, and metaphoric, symbolic, political, or actual death.[3]

Context makes a difference, especially for radicals. The key to understanding the context is diligently looking, listening, and learning. Context is embodied in relational learning.

It is of little wonder why politicians and law enforcement officials, in attempts to shut down mass movements, go after the leadership, especially the clergy. Tactics include an invitation to join the politician's team with the promise of reaping professional and personal benefits: "Reverend, I can give you a paid position, put you on a board, or appoint you to sit on a prestigious committee." Such offers are quite seductive and potentially divisive.

Radical voices have been silenced by offering the church a daycare center, grants, affordable housing units, relaxing the zoning codes to build a new facility, or the forgiveness of some debt. Under those rules, clergy must tone down or shut down their rhetoric and resistance. If you dance to the music, you must pay the piper.

I remember calling a meeting with the mayor of an urban city. The Black pastors agreed we were on the right side of the issue, and we would stand together at the meeting. On the day of the meeting, nearly all the pastors had a reason they would not be able to attend. Out of about forty-five clergy persons, only three came with me to meet the mayor. The meeting went well, even with a small representation. Later I asked my colleagues what really happened. "Will, we either work for the mayor directly or indirectly, or our spouses teach in the public school system. We need the health benefits, retirement plans, and insurances that our churches cannot afford to offer. It was made clear to us that we were not to show up with you."

Plan B: If such an offer is rejected, then keepers of the status quo attack the clergyperson's character. Financial institutions or government investigators are sent after you. Media are encouraged to investigate how money is spent at your church, by whom, and for what. Such practices are aimed to demonize you, label you a hypocrite or a cheat, and eat away at your following. The son of Adam Clayton Powell Sr. found this to be true when he became the pastor of Abyssinian and a United States congressman. Powell was charged with allegations of corruption in 1967 and was excluded from his seat.[4] This lesson is one of the many lessons learned by the Black church clergy leaders.

Plan C is the one I hear about most often from ministry colleagues. There are so many demands to bring about change in our communities. Clergy burn out. We are silenced by the self-inflicted wounds of doing too much without the collective to share the load. We try to juggle too many balls in the air. We drop some or grow weary from keeping all of them up in the air at once.

Worn-out clergy lie on my psychoanalyst couch expressing feelings of inadequacy. They question how to be responsive to the ever-increasing demands of social justice ministry.

Clergy spouses and pastors' kids often feel abandoned by the parent who is out to "save the world" at the expense of quality time with their family.

Armed with a seminary education and standing on the moral authority of our sacred literature, issues that clergy address can be at odds at times with the desires of the congregation. Socially responsible religious leaders are overwhelmed by the desire to address gun control, immigration, reproductive health, human trafficking, global warming, white supremacy, mass incarceration, violence, affordable housing, living wages, corruption, food deserts, crime, and a list seems endless: George Floyd, Trayvon Martin, Eric Gardner, Michael Brown, Breonna Taylor, Emanuel African Methodist Episcopal Church, Charlottesville, El Paso, Orlando Pulse Nightclub, Route 91 Harvest Music Festival Las Vegas, the Jersey City shooting, and so many acts of violence whereby the church is expected to react, comfort, and heal shattered communities. Any one problem is wearing. Clergy are often expected to address each one while maintaining the expected pastoral responsibilities to preach, teach, visit, administrate, and love their flock. Ministry is about relationships. How clergy respond to the challenges of seduction, finances, creature comforts, and crises are the faith-based leaders' take-home exam on relationships.

Leaders must resist the urge to be all-purpose problem solvers. Opportunists rush to every crisis to be quoted and capitalize on misery. Some leaders need to be needed. They relish being quoted in the press. They love their talking-head moments on television programs. In the desire to be important, one becomes spread too thin. Clergy cannot and should not attempt to do it all.

Stick to your knitting. Identify your limits. Develop leaders in your congregation and partner with colleagues you trust to share the load.[5] Recognize that resistance comes at a steep price. Ask yourself, are you willing to pay the cost of discipleship? If you are effective in the fight for change, status quo protectors will attempt to dilute or ruin your relationships with the members of your community and beyond.

Sacred literature warns religious leaders to expect such temptations and dangers. And history provides examples of what happens to radicals who challenge the status quo. Look at the disappearing journalists who wrote about the destruction of the rain forest. Note the violent end of life for Gandhi, Martin Luther King Jr., and so many others who were witnesses to what power brokers do to maintain their power and control. Do not be naïve. There is a cost to discipleship. Grace is not cheap.

## Your Context Is Unique

Radicals want to build a stronger, fairer society. The devil is in the details. What is unique about your context and situation? What are the important barriers, critical questions, historical realities, and theological perspectives to place on your radar screen in the struggle for human rights, equal rights, and social justice? This section digs deeper into these questions.

Usually, one size does not fit all. We are unique. Each context is different. One may find some similarities; however, each situation has variables that set it apart. The task is to examine and understand your own context by looking, listening, and learning.

The value of knowing your context became clear to the leaders of the Interfaith Community Organization (ICO) as we attempted to build affordable housing in 1989. We were trying to duplicate the Nehemiah Project, a process that had enormous success in New York City. Our thinking was the quality of life in neighborhoods improves when there is a strong core of homeowners united together to address common concerns where they live. We were quickly confronted by the reality that Jersey City is one PATH train stop away from New York City, but Hudson County, New Jersey, is not New York City.

Our goal to build affordable housing seemed noble. We had clergy colleagues and experts with a success record of building affordable homes less than a forty-five-minute drive away. Our team had every reason to believe we could duplicate the effort in Jersey City and other locations in New Jersey. We did not fully appreciate how one river, one train stop, and a change in context could spell success or failure. Context makes a difference. Know your context.

Longtime Jersey City residents bragged about playing on green mountains without realizing it was harmful toxic waste and seeing yellowish-green water in parts of the city. I went to visit church members. To my shock, there were green and yellow crystals on the walls in their basements, and some of the public schools had similar reports. Being from Harlem, this was a foreign experience for me.

Added to my learning curve was the substantial number of church members and their neighbors diagnosed with various cancers. Like any good pastor, I made hospital visits and called numerous agencies to understand the reason behind such a spike in cancer-related illnesses. In short, most of the responses from various agencies blamed the victims and suggested that lifestyle changes would produce better health outcomes. The heartless racist responses pushed ICO's lead organizer, Joe Morris, to use another strategy to find answers. Joe was a gentle, humorous, witty young white man from North Carolina. Like me, Joe enjoyed pushing the envelope and, more importantly, he loved to hold decision-makers accountable for their actions. He was a tireless researcher. Together with our team, he and I began tracking where people who had cancer lived. We made a note of the kind of cancers and what zip codes each cancer was found in. At the same time, Joe encouraged soil testing. More than a few times, Joe purchased kits and conducted a soil study personally. The bottom line: more cancer illnesses than not were environmentally related, not related to lifestyle issues.

Discovering environmental hazards in neighborhoods where poor people live and work is not new. Drive along the New Jersey Turnpike when the wind blows; in certain sections, the smell is undeniably awful. Chart where government employees approve incinerators, waste dumps, manufacturing plants that emit toxic fumes, and crimes against the environment. Aging pipes that leach lead into the water are usually found in poor neighborhoods.

When pitching our story to a popular Sunday evening news program, Joe and I were told that viewers did not want to hear about poor people with environmental problems. Instead, the program aired a story about a cancer cluster in a well-to-do area on Long Island. We were happy this dreadful situation was being exposed in Long Island but sad the television network did so at the expense of our findings. Learning that the land the mayor of Jersey City gave ICO to build two hundred owner-occupied, affordable homes was toxic came as a surprise (at least to us).

In retrospect, ICO's leaders, including myself, should not have been surprised. Portions of Jersey City were built on a landfill.[6] Research made it clear the ingredients in the landfill killed rats, roaches, and weeds. Hello! One of the many factors that made the Jersey City context unique was the history of this problem. Added to the known health hazard was the cover-up by government officials over a few decades. We at ICO were the stars in our own version of *Murder She Wrote* or *Law and Order*. Even though city and state officials and subject matter experts, were allies the cover-up was exposed. One by one, ICO held all the responsible parties accountable.

We had no idea that a few interfaith clergy trying to build affordable housing would find ourselves on the front pages of major newspapers, on television in Scotland, before governors, federal officials, and countless city employees. The British Broadcasting Company (BBC) sent a crew to interview our team. It became clear that our toxic environmental experiences and the resulting fights were duplicated throughout America and the world. Our insistence on pushing the envelope for a Fortune 100 company to clean up one hundred acres of toxic waste, specifically chromium, led to a federal law enforcement member, along with a high-ranking federal health officer, telling me, "Be careful! You are doing excellent work. Know that it has put Willard Ashley on the radar screen of people who can hurt you. Reverend, agents can plant drugs in your car, and even your mother will think you are a drug dealer. You are making the wrong people extremely nervous." Members of my church insisted that I travel with bodyguards, and I did.

ICO was simply local interfaith leaders trying to build affordable housing to strengthen disadvantaged communities and help hard-working families experience the American dream of homeownership. To a person, in our wildest dreams, we did not expect what we experienced, both the ups and the downs. Against this backdrop, we became very aware of the importance of research, beginning with knowing your context.

## Factual Information

For the discussion in this section, I will use the term congregation. You may substitute it with the term community or movement, depending on your needs. Begin your exploration into your context by gathering some basic facts.

### Exegete Your Context

In the same manner that one will exegete a text before teaching or preaching, radicals must exegete their context before going to war to bring about change. Many clergypersons have suffered career-ending damage because they did not first exegete their context before applying the lessons learned in seminary about social justice and ethics. Every congregation that shouts they are progressive may not be as progressive as advertised. Do your homework, or you risk getting burned and irreparably damaged by members of your congregation or community.

### Identify the Unique Characteristics of Your Context

What is unique or distinctive about your context? Is it geography, topography, demographics, political stance, history, culture, or a host of other variables? Ask congregants, colleagues, business owners, residents, law enforcement officers, firefighters, physicians, delivery persons, teens, elected officials, utility company executives, bankers, and anybody willing to offer their perspective. Take note of the repetitive themes. Own the uniqueness of your context.

Following the tragic events of September 11, 2001, an army of experts from Oklahoma City immediately descended on New York City seeking contracts to help heal the city. Each professional came armed with a successful track record of accomplishments following the Oklahoma City bombing. Out of desperation, some were given contracts in New York City without any critical analysis of the difference in contexts. One size does not fit all. It was, in some cases, the disaster following the disaster. New Yorkers quickly educated the out-of-town professionals about the city's uniqueness as the country's largest city. For starters, the United Nations is housed in Midtown. Downtown Manhattan is the home to Wall Street, the financial capital of the world. New Yorkers boast of two baseball stadiums within one train ride of each other. The five boroughs contain 472 subway stations,[7] which covers more than "665 miles of mainline track."[8] New York City hosts eighty-three museums.[9] There are seventy-seven police patrol precincts with approximately 36,000 police officers, according to the New York Police Department (NYPD).[10] CBS New York shows an updated map that there are 640 different languages spoken in New York City.[11] Oklahoma City is not New York City.

If not for the tragedy, it would have been funny watching out-of-town experts trying to convince professionals from Columbia University, professors from the major medical schools in the Greater New York City area, and an army of city-based local psychotherapists that they understood trauma and the best practices for healing in our context better than New Yorkers. I wrote about the concept in two of my books; I called it "the absurdity of arrogance." The first rule of consulting is going in dumb. In other words, you respect their understanding of the context, ask questions, learn, and appreciate that the people who have lived through the situation come with a valuable body of knowledge. Listen! Context matters. Know what is unique about your context.

**Know the History of Your Congregation**

Church history was not my favorite subject in seminary, even though my grades were excellent. Somehow, learning a mostly European perspectives on the development of Christianity while only minor lip service was paid to the remaining three-fourths of the world was not appealing. I recall my best friend raising his hand in class, asking, "It looks like the early Church Fathers and Mothers came from Africa. Is that correct?" Being the only Black students in the course, he and I looked at each other with disappointment as the professor responded, "Yes," and kept going on with the lecture as if our observation did not matter. Howard Zinn changed how I look at history. He made history about stories. History, in his presentations, was unfolding drama. He taught history as unsolved mysteries with the student as a detective. Zinn also caught my attention because he told history from the view of the marginalized and victimized. In his book *People's History of the United States,*[12] Zinn made it clear that it is crucial to know who tells the story and to dig out the context and their agenda in sharing the story. Clergy and clinicians see this in operation when siblings tell stories of their upbringing. Listening to the differences in how siblings remember and tell the story is as if you were talking about two separate households. Who tells the story, why, and how is important. After the date, time, and place, the rest of the story may be left up to subjective memory or be outright agenda driven.

Five years into my pastorate at the largest Black congregation in Jersey City, academic pursuits led me to the main public library. I had heard many stories about the development of Jersey City and our congregation's role in the history of the city. Seniors shared stories about how the church grew under each previous pastor. Pride exuded from the membership each year when the congregation's history was read during the church anniversary. What I learned during my trip to the library caught me completely by surprise. Going through the archives, I read about church officer suicides and scandals that somehow were never told to me, and I had asked. It was clear that years later, hidden stories still had an impact on the congregation. This information totally changed my understanding of the value of learning the histories of the congregation and community.

The lesson is simple yet profound. Be attentive to what is told and dig to find out what is hidden or kept secret. You will discover that the findings from your research can often take you places you did not expect or see coming. Carefully read the documented history of the congregation. Find articles about the congregation and their leadership. Compare notes. Ask questions, especially of seniors. Histories unlock a treasure chest of information.

How did your congregation start? What drove the founders to begin this effort? Who were the pillars? Draw a timeline based on years or other measures of time. Put on chart paper the history of your congregation or movement. Note significant moments and events to be flagged on the timeline, such as purchases, deaths, additions, celebrations, mortgages, address changes, significant fights, accomplishments, leadership changes, and watershed moments. Run a parallel timeline to chart what was going on in the community, region, and the world. Timelines offer a visual look at your history. Know the history.

**Review the Mission Statement**

Usually, congregations have a mission statement. If you do not have a mission statement, create one! It is well worth your while to be familiar with the congregation's mission statement. Read what it says and what it does not say. I have seen clergy undergo major trauma because they did not pay attention to the mission statement. The mission statement may be your first clue if the congregation has an appetite for social justice work.

Look at the history of the mission statement.
- When was it written and by whom?
- Can you document the process by which the statement was written?
- What was happening in the community and world when the mission statement was written? Does it match the tenor of the times?
- Did the congregation update the mission statement? If so, when and what drove the change?
- Does the mission statement reflect your experience of the congregation?

It may sound silly, but sometimes congregations are clueless about their stated mission. Planning a time to understand the church's mission statement can be an opportunity to agitate the leadership as to your current mission. You may question their new dynamics in the neighborhood, the congregation, or the world that are no longer reflected in the mission statement. The lived inconveniences, horrors, realities, and opportunities associated with the COVID-19 pandemic should drive congregations to revisit their mission statement. After a pandemic, what challenges and practical concerns need to be addressed? How does the new reality impact the church's mission?

I have watched congregations die when gentrification took place and the church's leadership did not see fit to review their mission. Similarly, some congregations have reported explosive growth due to redefining their mission with consideration to changes to the neighborhood. You might want to assign a team to talk to new neighbors and businesses that moved into your geographic area. Read the long-term plans for your community. Go to the library and read your local twenty-five-year plan. Sometimes it is online on the local government website. How can the congregation meet both current and future needs? What about your current mission statement speaks to current realities and future hopes? Review the stated mission of the congregation.

### Study the Theology of Your Congregation

What is the theological position of your congregation? Explore how the congregation's theology is the same or different from the theological stance of your faith tradition. You might discover a disconnect between the stated theology and actual lived, practiced theology. It is a good practice to read the documents, debates, councils, meetings, and conferences that shed light on the theology of your congregation and faith tradition. Know the theological stance of your congregation on politically charged issues, such as stem cell research, reproductive rights, LGBTQ equality, sexism, racism, and militarism, to name a few. Find what is on the church's website, in printed materials, and in sermons. Examine with a theological lens the sacred songs, hymns, and musical selections.

## Know the Political Context

I have had running battles with governors, mayors, and county officials. Often those fights included quotes in the media or at mass rallies. At times, a radical must make politicians uncomfortable for their voice to be heard. Remember, the action is in the reaction. One mayor posted in the media a threat to me to have public works dig in front of the church on Easter Sunday. His stated goal was to keep people from entering church on the holiest, busiest day of the Christian calendar. He was going to teach me a lesson about who has the power in his city. The headline read, "I AM CAESAR!" The local media, who agreed with my position in this fight, posted an editorial cartoon weighing in on the matter. Other clergy and the public reacted to the threat. We spoke to his donors and inner circle. Cooler heads prevailed. My organizer training and analysis of power taught us the value of knowing the names of donors, inner circles, campaign managers, political party chairpersons, and reporters. Know the political context.

In studying context for the purpose of activism, your success or failure may depend on the political stances within your congregation. What are the points of political tension and cohesion? Know who the elected officials in your congregation are, both past and present. Identify any political appointees. Discover who works for the federal, state, county, or city government. Examine what positions those individuals hold and how they came about those positions. People who have political positions in the congregation can be a blessing or a curse. Such individuals can share information and make you aware of programs, grants, and opportunities. The same people can be appointed to ask the pastor to tone down the rhetoric.

In one of my congregations, I commented on a county official during the Sunday service. This elected official did not like that I mentioned their name in the same sentence with a person on trial for murder. The political appointees and government grantees in the congregation asked me to apologize publicly. A relative of the elected official was an attorney for a nearby town. In a private meeting, the attorney suggested that I committed slander. I found it laughable, given the very public exchanges I'd had with other elected officials who simply threw their own rhetoric back at me and with whom I developed deep relationships of respect and accountability. My attorney thought it was an attempt on the part of the elected official to grab headlines at my expense. Given that my attorney had defended other high-powered activists, I was comfortable with his assessment of the situation and any risk or exposure on my part.

However, I publicly apologized. Someone in my family worked for a Fortune 100 company. The CEO encouraged me to apologize to the elected official. The Fortune 100 company did not want a senior executive's close relative embroiled in a fight with a local politician. Fast-forward. The same elected official was later convicted and served time in prison for corruption. The media beat a path to my door to ask for a statement on the day of the elected official's conviction. I said, "I am deeply saddened that the public trust was betrayed. Twelve jurors spoke. I pray for all the families that felt the impact of this betrayal."

Know the politics in your context.

## Learn the Cultural Landscape

Understand the unique features of the cultural landscape where you engage in ministry. Appreciate the challenges and advantages of the cultures, ethnicities, and patriotic pride. List the countries that are represented in your congregation. Honor each country. Celebrate together on the national holidays of their country. Offer educational material to the congregation to foster a deeper understanding of the various cultures sitting in the pews. Share stories, cultural insights, and food from each country represented. Spend time to understand how the cultural landscapes impact the world-view of your parishioners. Know how deeply the cultural landscape influences religion and spirituality. Sometimes the cultural landscape has more influence than theology or politics. This congregational cultural landscape exploration is labor-intensive, hands-on work. But the payoff is great!

## Comply with Your Local, State, and Federal Legal Requirements

Few things can kill a ministry or movement faster than failure to comply with governmental requirements. Make sure all your records are up to date. Be diligent about following proper accounting procedures and maintaining the guidelines for reporting finances.

If you receive grants or if large sums of money pass through your ministry, hire a forensic accountant. He or she will explore your finances for any sign of criminal activity. If your activism targets power players, be sure you can withstand financial scrutiny. Plan not for if, but when, they hit back. It is one of the areas of attack. Politicians, gangsters, and white-collar criminals have gone to prison because of unresolved IRS violations and questionable financial practices. Ministries have lost everything, not because they were bad people or greedy but because the proper paperwork was not filed, or government grant procedures were not fully followed. In fairness, if we are holding elected officials and others accountable, we must be accountable ourselves.

Times are tough. Do not cut corners or go cheap on accountants, lawyers, and people who oversee finances and ensure that you meet all legal requirements. History is transparent. Any radical that stirs up the masses to bring about change in a democratic society will receive a visit to investigate their finances. Bank on it!

## Critical Questions

You have collected the facts about your context. You have a greater understanding as to what makes your congregation tick. Now let us conduct a belief reflection. Apply what you have learned about your context to how it may impact your efforts to engage in activism. As this chapter comes to a close, allow me to lift some reflection questions. You may use these questions for a retreat, Bible study, leadership training, or clergy support group.

### About History

Historically, how have identities, teachings, or institutional power affected how people address social justice issues? How have stories been misused to support apathy and oppression? What does it mean to take back these "stolen stories" and reclaim power? Where do you see the hand of God in the history of your context?

Can new generations who have lost faith in traditional practices regain their forebearers' zeal, spirituality, and commitment? What kind of leadership style is necessary for this time in history? What do you want history to say about your accomplishments?

## About Religious Beliefs

What does your religious faith teach that strengthens your social justice work through community engagement? What specific sacred stories call you to engage in activism? What does your faith tradition put in writing through books, articles, pamphlets, and electronically to support or discourage social justice? What issues seem the most important to address in your faith? To what extent do we hold our teachings, beliefs, and values in common? How can we recognize and celebrate a shared calling that includes clergy from multiple faith traditions or become activists?

## About Institutional Transformation

How does one change and transform institutions? What have you learned working in your context, or what have you learned from what did not work? Identify the pockets of resistance to social justice and activism in your context. Who are the winners and losers if your efforts to transform your institution succeed? What outside forces impact what happens inside your institution? Stay focused. Rallies, marches, and staged events are needed if you are to be invited to the table to discuss changes.

## About Participating in Societal Change

What is the calling of ethical, spiritual, faith-based institutions to participate in the struggle for a racially and economically just society? What does freedom look like now and beyond? What cost are you willing to pay to bring change in your context and in the greater society? What writers, thinkers, journalists, bloggers, podcasts, or audiobooks are you reading or hearing that address the social justice issues that interest you? Who are the persons past and present that you look up to as champions of change? What are activists in other countries fighting to change? If you ever participated in a protest, talk about the experience. What is the hot societal change issue that gets your blood boiling?

### About Race and Racism

What is your understanding and definition of racism? Have you attended an "Undoing Racism" workshop or similar training? What have you read or listened to about race and racism? What is your experience of racism, racial disparities, white supremacy, and microaggressions? What would it mean to you for a Black person to be in charge or to be the public face or key figure fighting an issue? What will it take for you to embrace the fact that racism impacts all the isms? What is triggered in you when people talk about racism, white supremacy, and racial disparities?

## Step One

Congratulations, you took the first step. This process is an ongoing task. Again, the COVID-19 pandemic taught us that contexts change. Among other things, ministry has moved from an in-person experience to a video conference with virtual backgrounds. It is yet to be fully known how future contexts will be impacted.

Prepared with a working knowledge of your context, we move on to understanding conflict. What or who is the Goliath that is waiting for someone to step up and accept the challenge? What is the conflict that God has put before you to address?

### NOTES

1. "Los Angeles Riots Fast Facts," CNN, updated April 12, 2020, https://www.cnn.com/2013/09/18/us/los-angeles-riots-fast-facts/index.html.

2. Albert J. Raboteau, *American Prophets: Seven Religious Radicals*

*and Their Struggle for Social and Political Justice* (Princeton, NJ: Princeton University Press, 2016), 110–112.

3. Aldon D. Morris, *The Origins of the Civil Rights Movement: Black Communities Organizing for Change* (New York: The Free Press, 1984), 179–181.

4. PK Krentsil, The Moguldom Nation, "10 Things to Know About Political Legend Adam Clayton Powell," May 29, 2020, https://moguldom.com/223613/10-things-to-know-about-political-legend-adam-clayton-powell/, accessed February 14, 2021.

5. More on this form of self-care is found in Chapter 3.

6. For a history of this area, see: "The History behind the Former Roosevelt Drive-In Site," Jersey City Chromium Clean-Up, Honeywell International, http://www.jerseycitychromiumcleanup.com/background/history.cfm, accessed January 4, 2021.

7. MTA Facts and Figures, http://web.mta.info/nyct/facts/ffsubway.htm, accessed February 6, 2021.

8. Ibid.

9. Museums in New York City, https://www.ny.com/museums/all.museums.html, accessed February 6, 2021.

10. NYPD, https://www1.nyc.gov/site/nypd/about/about-nypd/about-nypd-landing.page, accessed February 6, 2021.

11. CBS New York City, Posted January 10, 2020, https://patch.com/new-york/new-york-city/new-map-shows-where-640-languages-are-spoken-nyc, accessed February 6, 2021.

12. Howard Zinn, *A People's History of the United States* (New York: HarperCollins, 1980).

# CHAPTER 2

# CONFLICT: EMBRACE CONFLICT AS PART OF THE PROCESS FOR CHANGE

## Conflict Is an Unavoidable Reality

Conflict is an experience most people want to avoid, but conflict is an unavoidable reality. Clergy have nightmares about conflict in the congregation. Ask any pastor; they can recall the church meeting from hell like it was yesterday. You have no idea what it is like to be in a nasty fight until you have engaged in a church conflict. Our sacred literature is filled with stories about conflict. Many of our expressions of faith were born out of conflict. Listen to our hymns.

Freudian free-associations with the word "conflict" tend to be filled with unpleasant memories. Patients lie on my psychoanalysis couch to discuss unresolved conflicts. Couples usually visit my marriage and family therapy office because of conflict in their relationship. Wars are fought over conflicts. Families and friends stop speaking over conflicts. On every street corner and in every suburb, town, and farm, conflict can be found. Try as we may, we cannot avoid conflict.

What if I told you radicals embrace conflict? Radicals understand conflict is part of the process for change. Radicals are not conflict avoidant. In fact, radicals believe a good conflict should not go to waste. Radicals use conflict to strengthen relationships and build mutual respect. This chapter is designed to help you push the reset button in your thinking about conflict.

Demands for social justice are quite often met with conflict. Radicals encounter outright refusal to meet what we think are reasonable demands. We find it preposterous that some human beings have problems treating others with respect, dignity, transparency, and fairness. For radicals, social justice issues are like wounds that do not heal unless they receive skilled attention. Thus, we cannot run from conflict because it makes us uncomfortable. The labels thrown at us in a conflict might be more than our egos can handle. Some may find it safer to be victims.

Radicals expect attacks, labels, propaganda, and the mischaracterization of our demands. Those in power rarely, if ever, concede without a fight unless it is the next move on their chessboard. People want to believe so desperately that leaders, government, institutions, and systems are all working for the public's best interest. Activists, organizers, historians, and social scientists have documented such is usually not the case. Ordinary citizens, so-called radicals, engage in conflict to bring about the changes we want to see in policies, practices, neighborhoods, communities, congregations, and the world. Thus, we butt heads with multi-national Fortune 500 companies, politicians, puppets, developers, lawyers, spin doctors, and systems that rob people of their dreams, take away their dignity, and diminish their humanity. Without constant pressure, power maintains the status quo. Conflict is unavoidable. Embrace it. It is part of the process to be heard and to bring about change.

## Define the Problem.
## Break It Down to Winnable Issues!

People in power do not take ordinary citizens seriously. The average citizen is not offered a seat at the table where decisions about their futures are made. Average citizens must push and push and then some for their voices and perspectives to be heard, respected, and incorporated. That is absurd—aren't we living in a democracy? However, there is too much money at stake. Elected or appointed officials have made too many promises to get into and hold office. Being at the seat of power is too intoxicating. People in power see the rest of us as mindless consumers whose only value is to consume and buy wholesale their agenda without question. The system is designed to rely on the "experts" to set the agenda and block out ordinary citizens' voices.

Power itself is not a problem. All of us want power. The first problem is what people do with their power. The second problem is what voices influence the people in the seats of power. These two problems create ideological, political, and practical challenges for most citizens. Our voices are silenced; that is the primary problem. The rest is just contextual variations.

This language about problems and power is off-putting to some. It reminds me of how grants are written: Here is a problem that we seek to solve with a grant from your institution or foundation. We stand with our hands out, asking the philanthropy to fund us. The approach starts with a negative looking for a solution. This chapter offers an alternative methodology by identifying how silenced voices rob citizens of their basic humanity and how radicals foster hope through understanding conflict, problems, and issues.

Problems tend to be giant, uncontrollable monsters that de-energize even the most optimistic personalities. Problems rob people of hope, leaving many to shrug their shoulders as if to say, "What can you do?" Embedded within each problem is a series of issues. When couples come to my office for counseling, part of the intake process is the question, "What brings you to couple's therapy?" Of course, I have had some concrete thinkers who said, "Our car. It's a BMW." However, most often the couple recites a problem. One of the common problems is communication. My task at that point is to narrow down the problem into manageable issues. What about communication do you find problematic? Once the bigger problem is pared down to measurable issues, the couple and I can track evidence of their progress.

People in power hate being held accountable by specifics, measurable benchmarks, and total transparency. Those in power see such requests as problematic. I have yet to meet the person in power who thanked ICO for posting a report card in the media on their progress, or lack thereof, on our demands. "Mr. Official, you promised to clean up this toxic waste site. Two years later, not one shovel has hit the ground." Action is in the reaction. This official garners a reaction in the media.

Radicals are relational. We want relationships with those in power. We want to share our perspectives on how to improve upon policies or positions after listening to hundreds of citizens in their homes, community centers, and hangouts. Radicals are not afraid of power, nor are we fearful of powerful people. We embrace such relationships as vehicles to bring about change.

## Conduct One-on-Ones and Host Relational Meetings

Relational meetings are not photo opportunities, nor are they sessions where you do most, if not all, of the talking and the good, well-behaved citizens must listen. Radicals are not to sell our latest idea or test the waters to announce a potentially unpopular decision. We listen more than we talk.

After a horrible mass shooting in a Jewish deli that rocked the Jersey City community, the governor called for a clergy meeting to listen to us. We were excited for the audience. Most of us voted for this governor, so he was among supporters. The meeting was set to last ninety minutes. Photos were taken. The national media praised the elected officials for being present. Each speaker slipped into their speech while I spoke with members of the family. There was one problem. After a line of elected officials spoke and smiled for the camera, there were only ten minutes left for clergy to speak at what was billed as a listening session to hear from the clergy. Even when promised a voice, we were voiceless.

Radicals, believe you have a voice. Your voice is important, and it is worth people's time to listen to you. But our first task is to listen. The best-intentioned leaders know it is one thing to create a policy and something different to see how it works on the ground.

There is a well-respected university in Manhattan that had a vision to host a conference to examine the plight of the poor in New York City. The leadership assembled a blue-ribbon team of experts to plan this conference. I am not sure how I made the list, but the leadership invited me to participate in the conference's planning. The ideas were flowing. The energy was high. We were proud of our efforts. I saw something strange about the diverse group of assembled planners but opted to keep it to myself; I thought it would be corrected at the next meeting.

The conference planners were good, well-intentioned liberals who did have a heart for the poor. Yet in spite of their lack of ill will, this observation kept bugging me. At the next meeting, more blue-ribbon participants were present. There was power in the room. I know people who are invited to these sorts of functions should be glad to be there and are supposed to keep their mouths closed. Years of experience taught me that checking a particular demographic box often gets one invited to the seat of power. But there seems to be an unwritten rule that such invitees are to be seen, not heard. Radicals, however, ignore that rule. We speak our minds, even when it makes the people who invited us think that they made a mistake to bring us to the table. Word may spread that it would be a mistake to include us in other such gatherings. Our hosts might think, "He or she thought we really wanted their input," when what was expected of us was actually "Shut your mouth. Know your role and shut your mouth," as the World Wrestling Entertainment personality The Rock would say. In these situations, we help check the boxes for political correctness or diversity, but decisions will be white culture dominant.

I raised my hand at the second meeting and said, "Where are the poor people? How can we plan a conference for poor people when no one here stands in line for food stamps or is a guest at a homeless shelter? In fact, most of us arrived at this meeting in luxury cars or took a modernized mode of transportation. Some of you in this room designed the welfare policies and put the systems in place. But you are not a recipient of those services. You do not know how it really works for poor immigrants, widowed Black women, or men with HIV/AIDS. This planning is all theory for us. We need poor people at the table as expert consultants." I made my point. It was totally ignored. I invested my energies elsewhere.

Relationship building involves respect and honoring what each person has to offer. The best way to show respect is to listen. The goal of relationship building is to listen, learn, and together discern what problems can be pared down into winnable issues and who can be developed as leaders. This strategizing is done through what organizers call one-on-ones or relational meetings. Carve out forty minutes or so for a give-and-take conversation with concerned parties to learn, listen, and share. Look for potential leaders in every meeting. Radicals show that we care about individual persons. Radicals communicate that we care about the things that are important to others. People who leave an impression usually make us feel important because they listened to us and demonstrated real compassion for our stories. Such souls communicate that our stories matter and that we matter. We feel and are validated. Our humanity is honored and respected.

What a change when much of society treats people as a problem, illness, case number, or customer identification number rather than as a real person, and business is conducted with an automated response assistant. We all crave human connection. Radicals develop meaningful relationships with a team of like-minded souls.

Let me be clear: solo actors on this stage do not last. Without a strong network of co-laborers and supporters, radicals are ignored, co-opted, placated, or assassinated (if not physically then politically or reputationally). A team of leaders, not a Lone Ranger out to grab headlines, is needed to win the social justice wars. Stop looking for the next celebrity preacher to be our savior. God called you to do something with a team of like-minded soldiers in the war for justice. Our sacred literature affirms the impact of teams working together on a common goal.

Seeking justice and fairness is war. If you are going into battle, it is an excellent idea to know the people who are in the foxhole with you. Before you take on issues, build relationships. One-on-ones help you learn about another person. It is an opportunity to know who the leaders are and to ask questions that help you understand the other person. Here are a few questions for examples: Tell me about yourself. What accomplishment gives you the most pride? Where did you grow up? Why did you choose this neighborhood to raise a family? What are some of the things you like about this community? How does your expression of faith give you hope and energize you? How does your sacred literature support your vision for your life and things that are important to you? What attracted you to the congregation where you worship? What stirs the most passion in you? Recall a time that you took a stand; how did it work out and what did you learn? Who are you reading or listening to on podcasts? Who are your favorite thinkers? In the conversation, look for connection, good stories, leadership, and energy. Most importantly, build a relationship. Be curious but not intrusive. Start with positives. The goal is to listen and to learn.

Most of us start out with hopes and dreams. Then something happens to confront our notion of what can be with the reality of what is. Going back to practical theology, Marvin Gaye's question takes front and center: "What's going on?" Describe what is happening. Where is the disconnect between your dreams and reality? There is a conflict, problem, or injustice that begs for attention. Define and describe the crime scene yelling for justice to be delivered. What has you angry enough to do something about it? People will describe a problem. Again, we listen, probe, and discover. Radicals start with the positives in one's life and spirituality. We begin with what are the positives in one's context.

Eventually, you will hear the usual litany: Drug dealers have taken over our neighborhoods. Children do not have clean drinking water. Women are being paid less than men for the same work. Schools are underfunded. Black men are being killed at alarming rates. COVID-19 has put race and racial disparities front and center. Jewish people, Asians, and those who are considered "the other" are being attacked. Rogue police use chokeholds on Black men until they cannot breathe, or shoot unarmed Black citizens. This horrifying list continues. It is where people hurt and have the energy to do something about it. Like a good physician, radicals are listening for the sources of pain, disease, and hope. We want allies in the work of transformation.

## Start with the Positives. Acknowledge the Pain.

Start positive. Build a foundation of trust and genuine care. You will get to the challenging problems and issues soon enough. One word of caution: Never go into a conversation thinking you know what drives people to want to act or give leadership on a social justice matter. Listen! You do not know what you do not know. Humble yourself. Listen.

The clergy in Jersey City thought we knew what the masses wanted. We clergy are trained professionals with our ears to the streets. ICO's full-time community organizer, Stephen Robinson, pushed the spiritual leaders in Jersey City to conduct one hundred house meetings and to engage in as many one-on-one conversations with residents.

We, as local clergy, decided to humor Stephen. He was new to Jersey City, and he was trying to establish his presence. He had no idea how connected we were to the heartbeat of this community. We conducted the one-on-ones and were amazed by the outcome. Wow, we discovered new things about the people in our community. Relationships were deepened. Clergy and community members connected with each other beyond the public image and visible persona. We saw each other as human beings with a story to tell. Clergy led house meetings where ten people in one neighborhood attended to share their stories and experiences. How humbling! We found out how wrong we were and how right Stephen was about listening and asking questions.

The number one desire for the residents was not safer streets without drug traffic. Instead, they wanted safe, clean parks where their children could play. Second, the citizens wanted better sanitation. ICO researched and found that suburbanites are not inherently cleaner than urban dwellers. This finding eliminated the mindset that urban residents are dirty and do not care about their neighborhood. The only difference was suburbanites have better sanitation systems in place.

Sidebar: We had a meeting with the head of an urban housing department. Armed with this same outdated elitist thinking, the department head suggested that it is impossible to make the changes we want because people in public housing are not paying their rent, and if they do it is late. When asked, the department head had zero statistics to back up his claim. We did. In the complex where ICO demanded changes, 95 percent of the residents paid their rent and on time.

Back to hosting one-on-ones and house meetings as a tool for research, building relationships, and identifying leaders. One senior said, "Just because we live in the urban jungle doesn't mean we do not want green grass and opportunities to have family gatherings in safe parks." Her quote stayed with us. It later became the basis to take on legal battles to clean up Liberty State Park and other Jersey City parks. She was right. Studies show that clean, safe parks that are accessible to all residents, especially in urban areas, are important to community health and stabilization.[1] It makes sense on so many levels. The lesson learned is to ask people what they want. Listen and validate their experience. Be curious. Honor another by hearing people's stories.

I will talk about analysis in later chapters. Right now, I simply want to impress upon you to listen. It is a golden opportunity to build relationships of trust, respect, and shared humanity. In listening, we discover. Where is the hurt? What are the webs of relationships? Who or what is keeping justice from being realized? What is being done for the next generation? Together we brainstorm what it takes to heal specific injustices and who has the power to bring about the changes we want. We begin to think out loud and to define what a win would be. Hope is established.

## Establish and Maintain Relationships
## Built on Mutual Self-Interests

Examine big problems to create measurable issues with benchmarks and goals. The Interfaith Community Organization (ICO) could not solve the drug problem, but we could and did close a few drug spots and usher in community-based policing to create safer neighborhoods. In our attempts to carve a big problem into winnable issues, our multi-faith clergy group invited Frank Lautenberg, senator from New Jersey, to go on a walking tour with us to what was one of the most drug-infested public housing complexes in Jersey City in the late 1980s and 1990s.

My task as cochair was to ask for a police presence during our tour with the senator. I spoke to someone high on the food chain in the Jersey City police department. (This is the same police department for which a mayor would later ask me to run as his police commissioner—an offer I turned down after profoundly serious thought and one that mayor and I laugh about today.) The response on the phone from the police representative was less than cordial. "Well, hotshot, you invited the senator; you protect him." My response was, "Sir, the Nation of Islam Black Muslims are only too glad to protect the senator.[2] I thought it is a bad look for your department. But the head of the mosque is standing right next to me. He is ready to do what is needed. May I have the correct spelling of your name and title for *The Jersey Journal* and *The Star-Ledger* for when they ask why the senator did not have police protection?" We heard the phone slam down.

Fast-forward to the day of the senator's visit. The neighborhood guys had already secured a safe space for me to park when I pulled up in my car. I waved at all the neighborhood lookout boys who had already spotted my car and knew I was Rev. Ashley, not someone undercover. Twenty minutes before the arrival of the senator, we heard strange

noises and looked up. Flying overhead was a police helicopter. We looked around and saw police with K-9 dogs.
Finally, we saw the police brass jump out of their cars to
double-check that everything was in place before Senator
Lautenberg's arrival. So much for "Hotshot, you protect the
senator"! What a difference a day made.

Senator Lautenberg arrived. We greeted, and before I could
say a word, the police took over the tour organized by us,
the interfaith clergy. Black Baptist preachers, especially me,
usually cannot shut up. For some reason, whether because
of the Holy Spirit or disbelief, I kept quiet and let the police
talk. Meanwhile, I walked alongside the senator the entire
tour. We reached a spot in the housing complex and an
elderly Black woman greeted the senator. She said, "Senator,
can you visit every day? We have never seen so many police
in this building." The senator looked at me and we groaned
and smiled. The police brass continued to lead the tour.

I was uncharacteristically quiet. One high-ranking officer said with pride, "Senator, we know who the drug dealers are. We know what days they make their pickups and
where the drops are made. We know the identity of their
supplier and where he lives." It took all my being not to
laugh. God, I got it. You kept me quiet, so I could set up the
senator to deliver the punchline. Senator Lautenberg looked
at me with a puzzled face. "Senator, I am not that smart. You
ask," I said with glee. The senator looked the police brass
dead in the eye and said, "If you have all this information,
why are these dealers still on the street poisoning the community?' Silence! Barbara Major, you were right; I must write
about this stuff.

Someone will read these stories and react as I did to *The
Jersey Journal* news reporter Earl Morgan. He was known
for being harsh on the clergy. Some things were factual, and
some were opinions. One day I had enough. I called to speak
with him. "Mr. Morgan, why are you so hard on clergy,

especially the Black ministers?" I asked. Without missing a beat, he replied, "Reverend, if the clergy did not do stupid things, I could not report it. I am reporting what you and your colleagues do. Stop doing stupid stuff, and I will write about something else." My response, "Touché." Point made!

Radicals want to hold others accountable and ask for transparency. We then must demand the same of ourselves and not be caught off guard when the media author a report card on our deliverables and actions, or lack thereof. Accountability goes both ways. We are accountable to God and the people who call us to serve. We are held to higher standards. It is in our job description written by God.

Building relationships to tackle power and the powerful takes on many faces. However, the goal is to listen, learn, lead, and love others as Jesus loved us. This approach to problems permits us to break them down into winnable issues. Trust, transparency, accountability, and respect go hand in hand. This understanding is another rule for radicals.

## Identify the Barriers that Divide Us

While building community capacity, engaging in social analysis, and developing leaders within our institutions and communities, radicals will encounter conflicts. This news comes as no surprise. Sometimes the tension comes from within our organizations and among interfaith colleagues.

The root of the conflict might be different theologies. We may find the tension between the exegeses of biblical texts, denominational positions, and political agendas that hijack attempts to engage in social justice. We may be tempted to play the "isms" against each other and fall into that trap, such as persistent calls to eliminate how race plays into ongoing social justice models. As the COVID-19 pandemic has exposed, the impact of race and racism cannot be escaped. We knowingly or innocently engage in typical divide-and-conquer tactics based on fear and old historical patterns.

Systems of oppression have been known to fight against each other. Ill-advised contests happen as to who has endured the most suffering. Kimberlé Williams Crenshaw, a graduate of Harvard Law School and Cornell University and a professor at the UCLA School of Law and Columbia Law School, is a Black woman internationally known as a civil rights attorney and a leading scholar on critical race theory. Her work attempts to document how systems of oppression work together. Crenshaw is also known for the introduction and development of intersectionality theory, which "is the study of how different power structures interact in the lives of minorities, specifically Black women."[3] Crenshaw examines how the interconnecting systems of oppression and discrimination impact women due to their sexuality, ethnicity, and economic status. Her groundbreaking work helps us appreciate how complex it is to build coalitions if we allow old patterns of division and fear to drive the bus. Early on, we must identify barriers that divide us and come to terms with those barriers. If not, power brokers will use those barriers to keep us from doing social justice work and interfaith community engagement. We will fight each other, and nothing will change.

Some years ago, a group agreed to come together around racism within the religious communities in New York City. Joseph Barndt, Roberta Samet, and Sandra (Sandy) Bernabei led the effort with the support of Mary Pender Greene. We met on 57th Street, at the Jewish Board of Family and Children's Services. The first meeting with persons from different faiths and various professions went swimmingly well. It was our feel-good moment. The second meeting started well, then the bomb that immediately broke up the meeting and our efforts went off. One of the Black Christians asked the Jewish participants about their stance on Palestinian liberation and statehood. We were done.

It took five years to attempt such an effort again. We tried again, equipped with new weapons to address the issues that divide us. After one year it is going well. This time around, we know better how to address the problems and issues that are barriers to working together to bring about change. It is important to put the problems on the table. Identify, own, and address the obstacles, or they will destroy your best efforts to unite, and business will go on as usual. Our coalition is starting with a look inside our institutions for racist tendencies and policies. We entitled the effort, "Taking It Inside."

We seek to build strong congregations and organizations free from racism before, or as, we take on the world. The work of building an antiracist, multi-faith coalition is difficult. My well-meaning, salt-of-the-earth, white co-laborers must be called out on occasion for asserting their white privilege in meetings, conversations, and events. Undoing four hundred years of conditioning is tough. However, once we agree to fight together to restore our common humanity, holding each other accountable is a foundational principle.

## Identify the Challenges that Scare Us: Cover-Ups, Collusion, and Cash

### Cover-Ups

Typically, cover-ups are designed so that citizens lose and the power brokers win. Any of us who lived during Watergate or read about it know that cover-ups are not some paranoid fear limited to the minds of conspiracy theorists. If cover-ups were only on the silver screen or the stuff that makes for good television, we would be happy. We know better. History has taught us that cover-ups are a reality, not fiction. Every branch of government has experienced cover-ups. Radicals have a nose for cover-ups. We smell cover-ups a mile away. Usually, our best weapons against cover-ups are investigative reporters, public information, whistleblowers, insiders, the Freedom of Information Act, eyewitnesses, watchdog organizations, forensic accountants, lawyers, allies, the court system, and an informed public who apply pressure to learn the truth. We learned from Watergate, always follow the money.

Our current slice of history has ushered in a new reason for cover-ups: violence! Unfortunately, we are eyewitnesses to an ugly side of America. Violence has become commonplace. Violent acts are performed regularly. Attempted cover-ups are exposed. The talking-head shows make it the feature story for the night. Local media show footage and document those guilty of harm to others. People tasked with protecting the public trust are disappointing the masses at alarming rates. We see on the news persons who feel justified acting as judge and jury without regard to human life or the impact on communities. Their attempted cover-up fails. The secret is out. The public reacts. Politicians panic. Anger builds. Police overreact. The media records every second. Your neighborhood finds itself on the wrong end of a national and international news story. The killing of George Floyd is an example.

Ironically, people who should know better forget there are cameras everywhere. Most people carry a smartphone with a camera attached. Urban neighborhoods have cameras planted everywhere from the corner store, to streetlights, to places law enforcement think we have yet to figure out. Police departments require their officers to wear bodycams. Young people equipped with excellent computer skills can find personal and public information on the internet. Electronics make cover-ups and keeping secrets more challenging.

Minority Uber drivers strongly encouraged me to run one or two cameras in my car. Record any traffic stops or interactions with others. Nothing is ever entirely deleted from the internet. Every day, someone asks, "How did you get that information?" Such a response does not deny the accuracy of the findings but shows wonder about what loops were not closed to prevent access to the evidence thought to be hidden. Radicals expose this kind of behavior. We want public relationships that are fair, just, transparent, and accountable. Cover-ups violate trust and create tension in our goal to build healthy relationships with power.

Cover-ups are sometimes used to discourage citizen participation or to ensure one group is given credit to the exclusion of another group. ICO worked tirelessly on lawsuits and followed up to clean up Liberty State Park. We met with countless scientists, lawyers, government officials, environmentalists, and local citizens. It was part of our efforts to free Jersey City of toxic waste. In addition to creating affordable housing, our goal was to have the courts order the polluters to remove toxins from public parks. In response to our one-on-ones and house meetings, we wanted to create safe and useful spaces for residents to engage in recreation and strengthen families with outdoor activities. Metro Field was filled with chromium and other pollutants. We asked the polluters nicely to please clean up the field but were stonewalled at every turn. The local newspaper posted a picture of an elementary school–age white girl sliding into home plate, kicking up toxic waste. The newspaper editorial took ICO's side, as did the public. Within a week, the polluter gave $5 million to clean up the baseball field. This victory confirmed we were on the right track to clean up parks for recreation and family use.

When ICO took on cleaning up Liberty State Park. our leaders spent over an hour with a scientist who insisted our position and research were wrong. Walking out the door, almost Detective Columbo style, we asked if the scientist would let his family play in Liberty State Park or if he would walk his dog there. He gave an immediate "Hell. no!" Our point was made.

ICO's name is attached to multiple court documents as plaintiffs. During this book's writing, a local resident who is an attorney shared with me binders and boxes of court documents with ICO named on each item. ICO won every case and appeal. When government officials and local interest groups retell the story, however, there is rarely any mention that ICO had any involvement in efforts to clean up Liberty State Park. Politicians and interest groups take bows for the clean-ups. Those same officeholders never admit either they, their predecessors, or their teams fought our efforts for decades. They continually cover up that organized citizens won multiple court battles to clean up the park. Some court orders have expired. Polluters, politicians, and elitist special interest groups think this is over. It is not! Legislation and enforcement are on the way.

### Collusion

"There is no collusion!" football owners famously said.[4] However, pick your favorite sport. Ever wonder why particular players are treated unfairly, be it a contract, or lack thereof, or Hall of Fame enshrinement? Deals are struck. Off-record agreements are approved. Power is consolidated and united. Only the naïve think that people are not blacklisted and blackballed. If you join the ranks of radicals, you take that same risk.

I am old enough to remember Curtis Flood. He played baseball for the St. Louis Cardinals. He was a three-time all-star and won seven Gold Gloves. Flood sued Major League Baseball and refused to be traded. Many do not remember that it was his courage and legal battles that opened the doors for free agency. However, it cost him his career. Collusion was obvious. Blackballed from baseball, Flood moved to Spain and was admitted to a psychiatric hospital before eventually returning to the United States and rebuilding his life. When Flood died, Jesse Jackson gave his eulogy and said, "Baseball didn't change Curt Flood. Curt Flood changed baseball. He fought the good fight."[5] Following the murder of George Floyd, professional athletes, like the rest of the world, began to react. There was something different this time. It was not the first time the police unjustly killed a Black person. Floyd's murder struck a nerve. Professional sports figures weighed in with their thoughts about race, social action, patriotism, and private thoughts were revealed. Black players in every sport began to share stories of the ways their sport colludes openly. Roger Goodell, the commissioner of the National Football League, offered a public apology for not listening to players earlier. He encouraged all players to speak out and peacefully protest.[6]

Michael Jordan pledged $100 million to fight for racial equality and social justice. Amazon and other companies posted on their website, "Black Lives Matter." Black players were vocal about how the media handles Black and white players. For example, if a white player returns to the bench yelling at their teammates to play better, they are described as passionate about winning. If a Black player does the same thing, the media and others brand the player as a hothead with anger management issues. This is a double standard.

Financial institutions, developers, and governments collude at times to the detriment of the public good. In 1989, national newspapers printed stories on how the financial institutions colluded with developers, real estate companies, and city inspectors to approve mortgages in Jersey City for houses filled with chromium and asbestos. Under a routine inspection those homes would never pass a fair test for hazardous materials. Fast-forward several years later and the scam was exposed in the media when residents tried to sell their homes to move to ones free of harmful hazardous materials. The financial institutions blocked those sales and cited the harmful materials in the basements and land. This is yet another sad story of collusion and cover-up. Banks were giving thirty-year mortgages for Section 8 HUD federal government-subsidized homes that had a shelf life of twenty years. Thank God Jersey City's new administration and the courts stepped in to address the injustice being heaped on working-poor homeowners. Collusion and cover-up do work together to dehumanize communities.

## Cash

This chapter is about conflict. I could not think of a better way to conclude such a topic than with a brief discussion on cash—money! At the end of the horror stories about collusion and cover-ups is cash. Money means power. Money can be used to help or harm people. It can be a vehicle to do good or a weapon used to control. Like power, cash is neutral until it is applied.

Max Stackhouse insisted that I read all of Max Weber's works and books documenting the early roots of Protestant capitalism when I was working on my doctorate. I aced economics twice in college. I understand capitalism better than the average citizen. I am not a communist. However, as a descendant of Africans who came to this land in chains to feed the capitalist hunger, I am in touch with the system's flaws. The ideology of capitalism finds a comfortable home in Darwinism. Such a partnership is rooted in a racist history.

I still want to embrace the idea that if a person has a dream, works hard, and convinces the public they have a better product, service, or idea, they can realize those dreams.[7] I applaud the star athletes and celebrities who use their income to create wealth, especially in marginalized and economically challenged neighborhoods. It is heartwarming to read about self-made billionaires with a socially responsible conscience. It is a pleasure to know that some wealthy people with power and more money than a person can spend in two lifetimes use their resources to help the planet and solve worldwide challenges. There are problems that only well-funded research can address. The sincerity and commitment of some wealthy individuals to make the world a better place are commendable. Then there is the ugly side of money: cash in social justice work.

This is a conversation I will never forget: My phone rang at exactly 5:45 p.m. on a weekday. A reporter from the *Asbury Park Press*, someone I had built a working relationship with based on several issues that resulted in news stories, was on the other end of the telephone. He said, "Rev. Ashley, we are about to put a story to bed. It will be the headline in my newspaper tomorrow morning and in other newspapers as well. It will become a national news story. We hear the Republicans are paying cash to Black pastors to suppress the vote in New Jersey." Puzzled why this reporter wanted me to know the information, I responded, "That sounds strange. But why are you telling me?" The reporter said in a hushed tone, "Because, Rev. Ashley, you are one of the pastors to be listed in the article we intend to print."

One can imagine my shock. After a deep breath, however, I was not surprised. This unscrupulous action was payback because several politicians spent time in jail due to information ICO had supplied. I also later learned that an ambitious local pastor was promised a position for his wife if he could "deliver Rev. Ashley." I knew that my voice and victories were making powerful enemies. As mentioned earlier, powerful people throw one-hundred-mile-an-hour fastballs at your head and hope to hit the target. This was their pitch.

The reporter then said the words that made our years of building a relationship worthwhile: "Rev. Ashley, this does not sound like you. I asked my editor if you and I could talk before we print the article. The article is going to be printed. I can convince my editor not to include your name with the understanding between you and me that if you lied and you did take money, I will come after you with every weapon a journalist has available."

Relieved and feeling confident, I responded to the reporter, "Fair enough. Thank you. Might I add, if such a thought ever crossed my mind, my father, Will Ashley Jr., will come out of his grave and whip my ass in the window of Macy's on 34th Street. Then he will make me apologize to the thousands of people who risked their lives so that Black people have the right to vote. He only had a fourth-grade education, but he knew the power and importance of voting. Now some inside information for you. I doubt very seriously any Black pastor took money to suppress the vote. If they did, the rest of the Black clergy would know. We have not heard rumors of new cars, mink coats for the significant other, diamond rings just because, or mortgages mysteriously paid off. And after Monday pastors' conference, each of us still will pay for our lunch. There will be no big spenders saying, 'I got this today.' It did not happen. Trust me."

The story was printed. It was national news. My name was never mentioned. It was rumored in some states the payoffs did happen. I know I did not participate. Money can be used as a weapon and a source of conflict for people on the frontlines of social justice. It can be used to quiet people, buy people, stop movements, fund activities, and corrupt. Like conflict, it need not always be wrong. It depends how it is used and for what purpose.

## Unresolved Personal Conflict

Allow the psychoanalyst to close this chapter with an alert. Sometimes the conflict is within yourself. You may be torn as to how much involvement is comfortable. Can you afford to see quotes from yourself in the media? Do you have the type of job and career in which activism is welcomed and supported? The conflict may rage inside of you as to how to respond. You must count the cost. Can you hold your peace? Is this your Esther moment? Have you been called "for just such a time as this" (Esther 4:14, NRSV). Being radical can jeopardize your livelihood and your life. It may be a price you are not willing to pay. It can cost you friendships. You may lose out on prestigious opportunities. Your greatest conflict can easily be the decision to get involved. You are Hamlet asking, "To be, or not to be?" How much publicity is comfortable and feels safe? Can you weather the worst-case scenario? What do you tell your family and friends? If you do not become involved, can you live with yourself? Conflict is unavoidable. It may come from outside forces. Conflict may come from within you.

## NOTES

1. Setha Low, Dan Taplin, and Suzanne Scheld, *Rethinking Urban Parks: Public Space and Cultural Diversity* (Austin: University of Texas Press, 2005), location 288 of 4458, Kindle edition.

2. The Nation of Islam is listed in the Southern Poverty Law Center as a hate group. However, quite often the Nation has strong relationships within the Black community and builds strong relationships with Black church leadership. Also, with the senator being Jewish it would not look good in the media that the Nation was willing to protect the US senator but the local police were not. https://www.splcenter.org/fighting-hate/extremist-files/group/nation-islam, accessed March 3, 2021.

3. Bim Adewunmi, "Kimberlé Crenshaw on Intersectionality: 'I Wanted to Come Up with an Everyday Metaphor that Anyone Could Use,'" *New Statesman*, April 2, 2014, https://www.newstatesman.com/lifestyle/2014/04/kimberl-crenshaw-intersectionality-i-wanted-come-everyday-metaphor-anyone-could, accessed February 12, 2021.

4. Dan Mangan, "Colin Kaepernick Reaches Settlement in National Anthem Kneeling Collusion Case against NFL," CNBC, February 15, 2019, https://www.cnbc.com/2019/02/15/colin-kaepernick-reaches-settlement-in-collusion-case-against-nfl-lawyer-says.html, accessed February 15, 2021.

5. Allen Barra, "How Curt Flood Changed Baseball and Killed His Career in the Process," *The Atlantic*, July 12, 2011, https://www.theatlantic.com/entertainment/archive/2011/07/how-curt-flood-changed-baseball-and-killed-his-career-in-the-process/241783/, accessed March 23, 2021.

6. Alicia Victoria Lozano. "Goodell Says, NFL Was Wrong Not to Encourage Players to Protest Peacefully," NBC News, June 5, 2020, https://www.nbcnews.com/news/sports/goodell-says-nfl-was-wrong-not-encourage-players-protest-peacefully-n1226361, accessed February 15, 2021.

7. Max Weber, *The Protestant Work Ethic and the Spirit of Capitalism*, trans. Talcott Parsons (New York: Charles Scribner's Sons, 1930; Vigeo Press Reprint, 2017).

# CHAPTER 3

# CHARISMA:
# USE YOUR GIFTS

## You Can Win

"Jersey City—Mayor Steven M. Fulop, the Jersey City Redevelopment Agency (JCRA), and the Department of Housing, Economic Development and Commerce (HEDC) announced an agreement for the construction of the first phase of Bayfront, the largest mixed-income development site in the region."[1] After thirty years of court battles, fights with elected officials, and offers to walk away, Interfaith Community Organization (ICO) won! At his press conference, the mayor announced plans to build 8,000 mixed-income homes with 35 percent of the project targeted as affordable housing. This project is the biggest undertaking in the region.

Father Geoff Curtiss, Ellen Wright, Myrtle Smith, Diane Maxon, Tony Aguilar, Joe Morris, Frank McMillan, ICO, Jersey City Together, and the federal courts forced Honeywell International to clean up Bayfront. Honeywell stepped up to the plate after losing their federal appeal and launched the massive clean-up of one hundred acres of toxic land.

Former United States senator and congressman Robert Guy Torricelli from Paterson, New Jersey, was appointed by the federal courts as the special master to oversee the massive clean-up. He was stellar in his oversight of the $400 million clean-up.

Sidebar: During the appeal process in Newark federal court, a star witness for us as the plaintiff in *ICO v. Honeywell International* jumped ship and joined the other side. He disputed his testimony from the first trial. I sat in the courtroom to hear their appeal. Let us just say a federal judge knows "the appearance of impropriety" when they see it and is not happy when that is brought into their courtroom.

Once the clean-up was completed to the federal court order's satisfaction, The City of Jersey City purchased the land (one hundred acres) from Honeywell International for $100 million. Jersey City Together, the current interfaith clergy group, encouraged the mayor and the city council to demand any proposals to develop this land allocate one-third of the units for affordable housing. At the mayor's press conference, he announced the first approved developers purchased sixteen acres of land from Jersey City for $26 million. They will build mixed-income housing.

Two developers were selected to share the first phase of the project. Their plan calls for 35 percent of the project to be designated as affordable housing units. This approach is in sharp contrast to the more widely used model throughout the state of 5 percent to 10 percent set aside as affordable units. Phase One will yield about four hundred affordable units. More land is available to be sold to developers who follow this model. Use your gifts! Trust God. Be patient when necessary. You can win!

ICO won our war because we were clear about our wants. We were also laser-focused on using our various gifts (charisma) to sustain a long fight. If your goal is to recruit followers or like minds to join your war, you must have clarity.

You must address six topics:

1. Find the root of the issue.
2. Be clear about the reasons this situation exists. In other words, who benefits if things remain status quo and who loses?
3. Identify any resistance to resolving the matter.
4. Chart the various relationships that impact your quest for justice.
5. Assess your resources.
6. Resolve to jump into this fight. This way is the effective use of the gifts (charisma) on your team.

Few stories capture this model as well as the biblical story about David and Goliath. Charisma is not about physical stature or a winning personality. Charisma is about being clear on your gifts and allowing God to use you.

## The Unexpected Appointment: David and Goliath

Few Bible stories are as riveting as that of David and Goliath. Many learned or at least heard of the story at an early age. The story has its beginnings in 1 Samuel 16. God rejected Saul as king over Israel. God was done with Saul as a leader and thought it was past the time to replace Saul's leadership. So, God makes an executive decision to select the successor to Saul from the family of Jesse, the Bethlehemite, and sends Samuel to Jesse's home. The stunned but proud father marches his sons before Samuel. As each son stands in front of Samuel, Jesse thinks he must be the one God has chosen.

Imagine how any parent might feel at this moment. "Greetings! Sorry to intrude on your day, but God sent me to anoint one of your sons to be the next king of Israel. If it is not too much trouble, can you bring all your sons in front of me right now? God has me on a tight time schedule. God wants this anointing done, like, right now."[2]

This is not a democracy. Citizens do not have to endure campaign speeches, attack ads, or debates. There are no visits to the local diner to shake hands with the candidate. Voters have been spared the need to hear the candidate's views on the topics that matter to them. Polls are not constantly updating the latest results. God alone votes on the next leader of Israel. God's vote is the only vote that matters in the story. It is for this reason that the criteria employed by God throws us for a loop. We humans use a different rubric than God.

Essential to understanding this passage in the context of *New Rules for Radicals* is God's instruction to Samuel: "Do not look on his appearance or on the height of his stature, because I have rejected him; for the LORD does not see as mortals see; they look on the outward appearance, but the LORD looks on the heart" (1 Samuel 16:7, NRSV). Jesse is puzzled that Samuel has not identified Saul's successor among his seven sons. There is one left but, come on, there is no way God is thinking of him as the next king. He is just a kid—handsome, reddish, but young, with all that goes with it. However, this is the one God anoints: David.

Charisma begins with the understanding that we radicals do not always pick issues. Sometimes they choose us. Problems find us. Most people do not set out to be a hero. Whether their heroism came from divine anointing, circumstances, emergency, or some crisis moment, many of the people we label as great did not have greatness penciled in on their calendar or life mission statement.

The next big event in David's story is familiar. The Philistine giant, Goliath, issues a challenge and demands Israel send a man to fight him. Panic sets in at the realization that Goliath is more prominent, more robust, and more skilled than anyone Israel can encourage to fight him. Vegas would suggest the odds are against Israel in this fight.

Radicals take on giants. The odds are stacked against

us. Systems, institutions, policies, practices, politics, laws, media, and religion are in place to maintain the status quo. Historically, the Black church was countercultural, radical, and prophetic. It took on giants—the major exceptions being opposition to women in senior pastoral leadership and our hypocrisy around LGBTQ issues. The practice of the Black church taking on giants is well documented. God speaks to radicals as God has spoken to Samuel. Do not be intimidated, nor impressed, by the size, appearance, reputation, technology, might, show of force, or position within society. Stand on the side of right, regardless of the odds. Such thinking is a radical, faith-based perspective.

## Root

People tend to react to symptoms and ignore the root causes. Many studies and experts outline symptoms of the more substantial challenges in society, but they usually fail to accurately and honestly identify the root of the problem. It is as if researchers and spin doctors are playing a shell game with the facts. Like good magicians do so well, they direct the audience's eyes to look away from what is taking place. Radicals encourage research that is transparent, factual, and filled with integrity. Radicals oppose research that is slanted to support an economic or political self-interest.

Radicals must be clear about the root of the issues we take on or the issues that find us. Gun control is not about trying to take away people's constitutional rights. Gun control, or the need to carry assault weapons, is not a failure of law enforcement to protect us (regardless of how overzealously in some zip codes). The root of the issue is gun manufacturers have not been held accountable, such as in the way cigarette companies were. It is clear which guns tend to be used in crimes and which weapons are used in hunting or to protect one's family.

David is engaged in a challenge against his distant cousin Goliath.[3] David rejects simply naming the symptoms and goes right to the root. Goliath's challenge is an attack on God. This is a test of faith. In any conflict it is important to be clear about the heart of the issue and what is at stake. This, more than charisma, draws attention, recruits support, influences your plan, and opens strategic options.

Radicals understand the root of an issue and the reasons for its existence. You must know how society works, who calls the shots, and the status quo's reasons. David correctly identified that Israel is afraid of Goliath. Better still, Israel, you have fallen short on the faith scale. You talked a good game, but when it came time to put your faith to the test, well, you came up short. There are reasons for behavior, be it psychological, political, historical, or how the system is run. Know the reasons.

## Resistance

Name a person who did remarkable things and never encountered resistance. Go ahead, I will wait. In my role as a psychoanalyst and social scientist, I expect and welcome resistance. Organized people with organized money will find resistance to any attempts to change the status quo. Mass movements can expect to be countered by the opposition. The teenagers and children who protested gun violence after witnessing it firsthand ran into resistance. It seems no matter how noble a cause, there will be opposition and resistance to change. Be clear about the resistance and why it exists.

Resistance takes many forms. In David's case, it was discouragement masked as care for him. "David, you are too young. You are not strong enough against this fighting warrior with many victories to his name. This giant is not your area of expertise. Stay in your lane."

## Relationships

David is a case study of relationships. He provides a wide range of bonds to examine and critique. However, for our purposes, let us stick to this story and the connections. As the story continues, David's relationship with Saul deteriorates (see 1 Samuel 18 and onwards). Unexpected succession transitions never go well. Leaders who do not plan on the day they will no longer be in leadership do a disservice to the institutions, organizations, and causes they worked to build. From day one, begin to mentor growing leaders who can follow in your footsteps. Discover those persons who share your passion and need to be developed, nurtured, and affirmed. This practice safeguards your work, encourages growth, rewards excellence, and keeps your ideas fresh. David understood his relationship with Saul. Better still, David realized his relationship with God.

David had history and experiences with God to draw upon. Keep it simple. What relationships will enhance your work? Who do you need to engage in a relationship with to accomplish your goals and objectives? Community organizer trainings suggest that leaders spend time meeting three new people a week and visit three old friends or current acquaintances a week. Know your neighbors. Meet the police chief and fire marshal before the rally when things are calm. Decide to lay out your plan and expectations. Always have colleagues in the media who know you and with whom you share information. Keep your attorney on speed dial. Ensure your medical team is aware of any changes, strange bodily reactions, or potential threats to your well-being. Being exposed to danger was not new for David. God allowed David to go into battle without fear.

## Resources

Saul to David: David, you have convinced me that you are

willing to go on this assignment to battle Goliath. I doubt how wise this is, but if you have a death wish the least I can do is appropriately equip you. Take my armor. It worked for me. May it do the same for you.

David to Saul: Saul, I value your benevolent offer. However, this is too heavy, it does not fit well, and these are not my weapons of choice. Saul, you mean well, but this will not work for me. I need to be more mobile, flexible, and nimble. Your armor is outdated, heavy, and difficult to maneuver in. Against such an opponent, quickness and the element of surprise are the tools needed to win. Your devices will not allow me to attack Goliath where he is most vulnerable. I am clear about what resources are going to lead us to victory.

The moral of the story: Strategic strikes can bring down might. Ask karate instructors. Vital to your success is to know your resources. Charisma is more than oratory.

## Be a Person or Organization that People Will Follow

People from many generations can recite verbatim the words to songs sung by Motown artists like Stevie Wonder, the Four Tops, the Supremes, the Temptations, or Smokey and the Miracles. Years ago, I watched a young group of kids walk down Harlem's 125th Street in awe. Looking in the window of a flashy clothing store, I heard the oldest of the kids say, "One day!" Those kids became known to the world as the Jackson Five. This chapter is about charisma. It is the successful use of your God-given gifts to change your community or the world.

One sleepless night, television remote in hand, I learned how Lincoln-Mercury inspired Berry Gordy to build the mega business known as Motown. In the documentary *Hitsville: The Making of Motown*,[4] Berry Gordy gives a firsthand account of how the assembly plant influenced Motown's business model. He took what he saw at Lincoln-Mercury and adapted their model to fit into his vision.

Berry Gordy was born on November 28, 1929, in Detroit, Michigan, during the Great Depression. He is the seventh of eight children. Berry had a love for music. Biographers note that at the age of seven, Berry exhibited an interest in writing songs. Ironically, Berry was kicked out of his high school music class. This one setback led to Berry dropping out of high school. He pursued a boxing career. By the time Berry turned twenty years old, he had won thirteen of his nineteen professional fights. Nevertheless, it became clear to Berry that music was a less painful road to success than beating up opponents in a boxing ring and being beaten up himself. Berry Gordy returned to his first love, which was writing songs. Berry was drafted in 1951 and put his dreams on hold. He served in the Army and earned his GED. By 1953 Berry Gordy was married with a family. In 1955, Berry was hired to work in the Lincoln-Mercury assembly plant.

Here is where the story becomes quite interesting. Putting upholstery in cars might seem like a monotonous and dead-end job. In fact, Berry's lessons at the assembly plant became his post-secondary education and the inspiration for building a multi-billion-dollar corporation. The job gave Berry more than just a steady income and time to write songs. It was at the Lincoln-Mercury plant where he learned production, sales, marketing, distribution, legal, and presentation. Berry understood that these were the elements of a successful business.

Berry made a decision that did not sit well with his wife: he gave Lincoln-Mercury his notice of resignation. He instead wanted to focus full-time on his music. The friction over his decision led to marital separation. This decision was dreadful for Berry's personal life, but what a gift to the lovers of rhythm and blues (R&B) music and the world.

Through a series of events, Berry Gordy met the manager of one of my favorite singers, Jackie Wilson. Growing up unaware of Jackie Wilson's personal life, I wanted to be like him. He was a sharp dresser from head to toe. His voice was soothing. On stage, he was a great performer. And equally important for an impressionable teenager at the time, the ladies swooned when Jackie flipped his hair and moved his body in those tight-fitting suits.

Berry Gordy wrote three hits for Jackie Wilson: "Reet Petite," "Lonely Teardrops," and "To Be Loved." With this success, Berry started his own music publishing company. It did not take him long to realize he must operate his own company to make real money. Biographers footnote that Berry borrowed $800 from family members. With borrowed money, Berry Gordy started Tamla Records on January 12, 1959. Berry used a house on West Grand Boulevard in Detroit for his headquarters. In 1960 Motown Records was incorporated. The rest is history.

## What Is Your Gift?

Like David, Berry Gordy used his charismata (God-given gifts) to create a once-in-a-lifetime situation. This combination of charisma and business knowledge became the foundation for the success of Motown. You may not be the next Berry Gordy. But you can be the next success story in your skin.

Charisma is more than a charming personality and a winning smile. In short, charisma is about your gifts. When pitching this book to another publisher, I wanted to use David as an example of charisma. I remember hearing from a few people, "Most of us lack the charisma of a David." Usually, that response was followed by a list of David's physical attributes, musical ability, and strategic prowess. Often, I responded, "But God did not ask you to be David.

There was only one. You missed the point. God enlists us to use the gifts God gave us and trust God for the results." Therein lies the charisma of Berry Gordy, David, and a host of other successful people.

We tend to start as invisible people. The public has yet to know our name. At some pivotal moment, God taps us to use our gifts. We respond—gifts open doors. Our gifts are put on display and create a desire for others to follow our lead. That is charisma. Be you and let God shine the spotlight. Did not Martin Luther King Jr. admonish an audience to "be the best street sweeper you can be"?[5] Okay, that's all for the mini-sermon. Use your gifts. That is the biblical understanding of charisma.

Our major challenge is knowing our gifts. There are the biblical lists of gifts. Self-help seminars, webinars, and vocational coaches offer their lists of gifts. Psychologists administer tests to assist in the identification of gifts. There are numerous books and online tools that provide a gift assessment. Some suggest it is good to assess your gifts at the start of your ministry and at mid-career. There are organizations around the US to help with that process, like the Center for Career Development and Ministry, which is based in New England but helps clergy and lay leaders from Maine to Texas. I am one of their vocational coaches. Discover, confirm, and affirm what your gifts are.

If you are going to engage in the fight for social justice, learn what gifts you bring. Such fights may not be your gift. To pursue it anyway leads to frustration, feelings of defeat, depleted energy, and even more. My dad died thinking I was Major League Baseball material. My sisters and I learned after his death that he played in the Negro leagues under a different name. Jackie Robinson was a cousin on my dad's side of the family. I loved playing the game. But it was clear to me, it was not my gift. I could smack curveballs and low-hanging sliders out of the park. But fastballs thrown inside over ninety-five miles per hour is why I am authoring books and not living in some mansion as a retired former Major League Baseball player.

## The Revolution Still Will Not Be Televised

What is the role of charisma in social engagement? Only a few will qualify if we reduce charisma to smooth, golden-tongued oratory filled with charm and wit. However, if charisma is about using one's gifts, the door is wide open in multiple ways, including participation in social justice. A host of others are needed to win the social justice battles.

Charisma in social engagement is about discipline and teamwork. The arduous work of social engagement is not conducted in front of television cameras or before mass crowds. That is the sexy stuff people associate with charisma. It is easy to lift up the orator who comes to town, says the right things, strikes the right notes, charms the crowd, and leaves. Radicals are left to do the demanding work.

Gill Scott Heron is still correct, "The Revolution Will Not Be Televised."[6] Mass demonstrations, protests, marches, and arrests (both symbolic and actual criminal activity) make headlines and provide material for hours of television viewing. What is not seen on television are backroom negotiations with mayors, police chiefs, prosecutors, and governors. Lost to public knowledge are countless meetings with city officials, state cabinet members, reporters, lobbyists, and aides who write the legislation. The work of change happens when policies, practices, laws, and new behaviors are in place. The sexy protest events get attention. Most people mean well but lack the strategic understanding that public protests are part of a process and not an end to themselves. Protests open a closed door to announce, "Now that I have your attention, can we talk?"

Protests, marches, and rallies are a show of public dissatisfaction and expressions of emotion. People in power look at those like town halls or school board meetings. "Thank you for sharing. It is 11:00 p.m. and time to shut down public comments. Have a great night." The bottom line is nothing changed. However, if the action is in the reaction, follow-up and demands must come immediately after the protest march or rally. Secure one thousand notable interfaith leaders' signatures on a letter from the same state or region. Ask for and receive a meeting with an elected official. Set measurable goals and results. Your voice will be heard.

Allow me to repeat that such an effort requires discipline and teamwork. Charisma is knowing how you fit into the grand scheme of an action or campaign. It is knowing your gifts and being content to do what you do best to move the agenda. Social justice is not about you! It is bringing about change. Follow the planned, agreed-upon presentation. Be prepared. Do your homework. Heed this word of warning. Gifts can be abused and used to harm people. Charisma can be manipulative. Dangerous minds control the masses by the misuse of their charisma. Your gifts are easy to abuse. Victims line the offices of psychotherapists; some soul misused his or her God-ordained charisma. Use your charisma wisely and with the utmost integrity. Do not seek to be the next David or Berry Gordy. Use your charisma, your gifts, to be you.

## NOTES

1. "In Wake of Pandemic, Jersey City Moving Forward with Largest Mixed Income Housing Development in Tri-State Region," Mayoral Initiatives, City of Jersey City, https://innovatejc.org/in-wake-of-pandemic-jersey-city-moving-forward-with-jersey-city-largest-mixed-income-housing-development-in-tri-state-region/, accessed, June 2, 2020.

2. "Samuel: God Chooses a King," Sermons4Kids, https://sermons4kids.com/god_chooses_a_king.htm, accessed on February 14, 2021.

3. Yaakov Elman, *The Living Nach Early Prophets: A New Translation Based on Traditional Jewish Sources* (New York: Moznaim Publishing

Corporation, 1994), 227.

4. *Hitsville: The Making of Motown*, written and directed by Benjamin Turner and Gabe Turner, aired August 24, 2019, https://www.imdb.com/title/tt6733446/, accessed March 23, 2021.

5. Judy Kuriansky, "Martin Luther King Jr. Words of Wisdom: Apply to Your Life," HuffPost, January 20, 2014, updated March 22, 2014, https://www.huffpost.com/entry/martin-luther-king-jr-wor_b_4624747, accessed February 15, 2021.

6. Gill Scott Heron wrote and first recorded this poem in 1970.

# CHAPTER 4

# COMMITMENT: AGREE TO ENGAGE

## Three Cultures of Response to Public Challenges

As mentioned earlier, Mike Gecan helped me throughout my ministry. He assisted me once again during a crossroads moment in determining the title and direction of this book. Mike said, "Will, you earned the right to write what you want. Close your ears to everyone else." He followed up on his words of encouragement by sending me a chart outlining the three cultures of response to public challenges.

Most of this book is focused on long-term community organizing. However, it is crucial to note and know there are other strategies for public challenges. Not everyone is able to commit to organizing for power, nor is it their interest. Furthermore, the headlines call to our attention some situations and moments that require immediate action.

The three cultures of response to public challenges are service, mobilizing, and organizing. Allow me to share briefly about each one.

## Service

The focus in a service response is addressing individual needs. Often the response is discreet. Service providers respond by creating programs. In economically challenged zip codes, there is no lack of programs. The recipients of these services are called clients or customers. Staff are seen as providers or responders. The executive director of a program is graded on his or her effective administration and competence in raising money, securing grants, supervising staff, working with the board, and giving birth to innovative programs. This model is attractive to churches that house the programs or benefit financially through the rental of space or jobs for their members. In this model, the pastor's role is to check practices, compile practitioners, coordinate partnerships, and catalog problems.

## Mobilization

Some incident confronts the public. There is an outcry for justice. The community demands an immediate response. Urgency fills the air. The headlines underscore the situation is a crisis. Media make the incident their lead story. There is a flurry of actions. Calls are made to elected officials. The days are filled with emergency meetings, texts, rallies, protests, speeches, and campaigning. Technology and social media have become the means to deliver the message. Innovative means of communication allow quieted voices to freely articulate positions without any hindrance and little to no censorship. The moment is punctuated by symbolic presence and rhetoric. Promises are made to investigate this horrible situation. There are calls for peace and pleas not to harm property or people. The public is angry for the moment. Changes to policies, practices, and laws are promised. Elected officials appoint an expert or committee to oversee changes. However, the systems of oppression are rarely, if ever, touched. Usually, in a few weeks, life goes back to normal and stays that way until the next incident. History repeats itself.

What congregations and communities expect from their clergy and leaders in these situations is a pastoral response: help in the crisis, healing in the community, and hope in the circumstance. A community leader's stock immediately goes either up or down depending on how these pastoral needs are handled during a crisis. The challenges that can make or break the outcome include but are not limited to historical tensions, feelings, misinformation, opportunists, and cultural humility.

### Organizing

Community organizing is the model represented in this book. In summary, this model relies on organized people with organized money to build power. Leaders engage their membership. Learning and teaching are ongoing. Actions are assessed based on reaction and effectiveness, and their contribution toward leadership development. Scouts are continually looking for leaders. The tools are individual meetings, trainings, power analysis, action, and evaluation. Leaders are encouraged to resist distractions. Remember the slogan, "Keep your eyes on the prize." Radicals are constantly scouting to recruit others to this brand of response to public challenges. This is the model that best addresses systemic issues and institutional racism. The starting point is understanding there is no quick fix. However, we hope to change our communities and impact the world, organized people with organized money who act with controlled anger, are needed.

## The Devil Is Real and Hangs Out on My Block

Commitment begins with the decision to become involved in issues that matter to you. Until adulthood, my sisters and I attended Catholic Mass at the urging of our mom and our maternal grandmother. There was not one Sunday that the Ashley kids missed Mass. We prayed before every meal and saying our prayers before going to sleep for the night was a mainstay. I watched my dad pray in private; he no longer attended church. Religion played an influential role in our family. I received my first call to the ministry at the age of seven on a visit with my grandmother to a Catholic retreat center in Lancaster, Pennsylvania. But we did not have a well-thought-out theology about evil or demons.

My neighborhood was cozy. The police knew the kids and our parents by name through the Police Athletic League (PAL) and community-based policing.[1] We played stickball and touch football in the street. Hitting the rubber ball the distance of three sewers usually was a home run. Handball kept us occupied for hours. We were busy in the winter climbing the snow hills and enjoying friendly snowball fights. During my early teenage years, the older guys called me "Foots." I wore size 13 shoes at an early age; it took a while for the rest of my body to catch up with my feet.

The neighborhood felt safe. Neighbors looked out for each other. We were a caring community. We celebrated Joe, who was in medical school. Audrey Smaltz made us proud; she went from being a fashion model to running couture shows in Paris. Neighbors often spotted the original Temptations with friends from our block. Muhammad Ali rang my doorbell once by mistake, looking for our neighbor one floor above. Famous actors and singers lived down the street. David Dinkins, who became the first African American to serve as mayor of New York City, gave free tennis lessons. We played basketball with this young center named Lew Alcindor from Power Memorial High School; he later changed his name to Kareem Abdul Jabbar. Guys from the world-famous Rucker Park basketball tournament and the National Basketball Association (NBA) played with us in the schoolyard courts. I dunked on the legendary Herman "Helicopter" Knowings in a pick-up game. Yes, basketball fans, I paid for that moment of joy. As one would say in basketball terms, he broke my ankles before he dunked on me backward. It was friendly. We were friends until his untimely death.

It was a great neighborhood to raise kids, learn the culture, grow up, and love your skin. The joys of the late 1960s became a distant memory as I entered my late teens. The cozy neighborhood gradually transformed. Our block slowly changed into one of suspicion, corruption, drugs, gangs, and white flight. A teenage club opened on our block called the Devil's Inn. This was much different from the well-chaperoned dances held at The Chapel of Intercession at the Episcopal church, the Devil's Inn lived up to its name. Teenagers from all over the city came, drank, drugged, engaged in sex in hallways or alleyways, and regularly robbed my neighbors and friends.

Rumors suggested that a local crime family bankrolled the club, and the police looked the other way. This was a precursor to the New York City police scandals in the 1970s through the 1990s. In 1994, my old neighborhood was known as the cocaine capital of New York City. Thus, such a rumor was easy to embrace. The media called the local police precinct "The Dirty Thirty." My family had experienced the pain of corrupted police officers. I witnessed police shake down Mr. Ira, our neighborhood number runner. Police also shook down my father, who ran numbers in Harlem in between driving a cab or working in the shipyards. My godfather, Brad Brewer, was a police sergeant in the Bronx. Drug dealers gunned him down. We learned his police partners sent him in first on a drug bust while they stood back. The partners' action allowed the drug dealers clear, open shots. Brad died because he would not accept the bribes. That day, Blue Lives did not matter.

These factors made the rumors surrounding the Devil's Inn believable. We were convinced as a neighborhood that demons were real, and they hung out on our block. The tipping point was when one of the well-respected, hard-working parents on our street was shot by a teenager who was leaving the Devil's Inn. This father was simply throwing out the trash when confronted by a gun-carrying teen who shot him.

Local organizers, public notaries, politically connected advocates, community activists, and the community-minded police officers helped the concerned residents. Together, we strategized and organized how to close the Devil's Inn regardless of who owned or protected it. And we were successful. The concept of the power of organized people with organized money intoxicated me. This victory to close the Devil's Inn was an example of radical behavior. The experience reinforced the notion that voiceless communities have a voice if organized to act.

This lesson on what can be accomplished against high odds stayed with me throughout my life. This gave me an example of what people working together in a community can achieve. Commitment and courage became real to me. What will it take for commitment to be real for you? Can you be courageous enough or so angry that you risk it all? How will you answer the call from God?

## "Who, Me?": The Call

A sense of call is important in the Christian tradition. Standing before an ordination committee, a candidate is probed, "Tell us about your call to ministry." Seminary professors ask students to describe their call. There is this sense that God personally asks a person to hit the reset button, that they receive an open invitation from God to go on a new journey. God is not looking for spectators. Instead, God asks humans to participate in the unfolding story of divine justice. We who are called look in the mirror. Our sins are before us. Puzzled, we ask God, "Who, me?" What does commitment look like in the current realities of America? What are individuals and institutions being called to do? Communities of all hues feel the impact of violence, hate groups, divisive politics, mistrust, scapegoating, ignorance, historical amnesia, and the unchecked radicalization of angry white males. Commitment is not the same for all. The late Benjamin Hooks, pastor, and executive director of the NAACP told this story: There was a bunch of civil rights workers marching past a farm. The farm animals said to one another, "Look at their commitment. We are proud of those civil rights workers marching in this southern heat and risking their lives. Let us do something to show our appreciation. How about we make them breakfast?" The cow spoke first: "That is a great idea. I will provide the milk." The chicken chimed in, "Let me produce the eggs for their breakfast." The goats boasted, "We can give you some cheese for those eggs." The farm animals noticed the pig was quiet. The cow shouted out, "Hey, pig, what are you going to give for breakfast?" There was a pause and a sigh from the pig. Finally, the pig uttered, "Everything you have offered to make breakfast is a contribution. Anything I can give for breakfast would be a sacrifice." There are various levels of commitment. Is your commitment a contribution or a sacrifice?

Given my family's history and my southern parents, I was born a radical. It is in my DNA. My parents raised their three children from the 1950s to the 1970s in New York City. I am the oldest and I have two sisters, four and eight years younger than me. We lived in a five-room apartment on the fourth floor of a walkup in Washington Heights. Most of our activities and family gatherings took place in Harlem. Dad had a fourth-grade education. Yet I am not being overly romantic about our upbringing when I say he remains one of the smartest men I have ever known. He was wise beyond his formal education. He read several newspapers every day and often grilled my sisters and me about current events. Standing at 6'2" tall and weighing 275 pounds, Will Ashley Jr. knew how to use his size to comfort and confront. Dad was a proud man. His closet was filled with custom-tailored suits, white shirts, designer ties, overalls, and his well-worn khaki pants.

Ask anybody about my dad; they will tell you he was a charmer. Any kid who did not have a father or was considered a behavior problem was taken on by my dad as a project, often with fantastic success. Our father's practice of being a dad to those without a male role model, especially the neighborhood "bad kids," also gave me and my sisters protection from being bullied. "Leave Mr. Ashley's children alone," was the word on the street because our dad treated all souls like family.

Our father's limited formal education reduced him to be a number runner, short-order cook on Amtrak, taxi driver, welder, and repair person. The family lived well. The refrigerator was always full. The kids dressed like we lived on Fifth Avenue or in Beverly Hills. It was only during a work layoff from the shipyard[2] that we were on welfare for a brief time.

Welfare was a temporary solution, not a lifestyle. My father made me go with him to stand in line to pick up our federally funded food supplies. He asked me how it felt standing in the welfare line. "What are you seeing on the faces of the people passing by?" he said. The looks were not comfortable, and I hated being in the welfare line, however necessary it was at the time. Dad said, "Hold those feelings inside. Remember what this feels like for you. Stay in school. Get your education. Hope you never have to be in this line as an adult. Remember those who must stand in this line to eat. Help those souls find jobs to be able to walk away from the shame line. Be an advocate. Activism is in your blood."

To their credit, our parents checked my and my sisters' homework every night, attended all the parent-teacher meetings, gave us summer reading assignments, and made us regular patrons of the public library. I remember my parents telling a teacher, "Our son needs more homework." The teacher responded, "Willard thinks I do not know that he does his homework in school before we dismiss the class." My parents saw education as the ticket off the welfare line for their children.

Read the call stories in the Bible. The biblical characters seem fully engaged in other work as the voice of God utters, "Come." Usually, the response is a form of "Who, me?" The person being called activates their bargaining skills. "God, you have the wrong resume. My qualifications do not match the job description. For the record, I am also busy right now. Even if that was not the case, my anger management skills need a lot of work. Honestly, this is not on the to-do list. There must be stronger candidates than me. And what are you offering to me? God, your offer is a big ask given you want me to go to destinations that are unknown to me."

God addresses us. Our task is to be attentive to the voice of God. Distractions abound. Reasons to turn a deaf ear to God are bountiful. The dangers of responding are real. God sends us to hazardous places. Obedience challenges us. Working for God has built-in vulnerabilities. Read the prophets. People are stubborn. Anxiety runs wild. Pharaoh-types demand total loyalty. Voices to the contrary do not fare well. Being a prophet is scary stuff.

You cannot and should not be prophetic without help. You need a community of supporters to stand with you. Justice is rarely, if ever, won standing alone. It is an honor, and it is also scary. God asked you to partner in social justice work. This work is a big commitment. Your response to being called is an exercise in trusting God.

After two years of college and three years of working on Fifth Avenue in New York City, I found myself in a training program at JCPenney in response to a blind ad in the *New York Times*. In the 1970s, JCPenney's corporate offices were in New York City across the street from the Hilton hotel. The management placed me as an assistant buyer in women's hosiery, which at that time was a $100 million subdivision. JCPenney had 1,600 stores with varying needs. Our subdivision was tasked with filling all the stores with geographically appropriate hosiery, promotional materials, and support. Our offerings ranged from heavy, striped socks sold in colder regions to ultra-sheer pantyhose for evenings out on the town.

Working at JCPenney deepened my understanding of commitment, power, and organizing. I learned the power of the pen. "We do not yell or scream or call people by names. We are polite and respectful, and we appreciate that our vendors, employees, and customers have choices." My boss, the senior buyer in hosiery, shared those words of wisdom with me my first day on the job. It was unheard of, but I could sign contracts as an assistant buyer. What a learning experience to sign contracts up to $2 million. Here, I discovered how a policy change could impact so many lives, or how the refusal to sign a contract could close a small-town busines by eliminating work at the factory. While Mr. Penney was alive, I learned that you can be ethical and still turn a profit. He and his immediate successors met with other CEOs regularly to pray and study the Bible.

I was single in New York City, father to a son, earning good money, hanging around fashion models, flying Leer jets out of Teterboro Airport, eating in the best restaurants in New York and New Jersey, attending Knicks games in the celebrity section, and blessed that my parents and siblings were able to share in the success. The morning after a date with a supermodel, God asked me two questions: "Is this why I saved you from the dangers and horrors of the streets of New York City? Is this why your mom gave birth to you after three miscarriages?"

The questions were my "Who, me?" moment. God had twice encouraged me to accept a call to ministry. Something felt different this time. Saying "no" did not feel like an option. I remember telling family and friends about this call to ministry. Each person replied, "You are the only one who did not know you were called to the ministry. Glad you finally read the memo."

The corporate world taught this guy from Harlem all God felt I needed for my commitment to ministry. It was time to retool. God wanted to send me to another classroom to learn how to be radical in ways I had never imagined. People of faith, Christians, work out of a sense of call. God kept calling until I finally picked up the phone. How does one hear a call? Your call story may not be dramatic. God may use a small, still voice (see 1 Kings 19, especially verse 12). Your call may come in anger as you see certain conditions or witness injustices. Or perhaps you gave a talk on a special day at your house of worship and people said, "You have a gift. You should preach." Again, one size does not fit all.

How do clergy, congregations, communities, and global leaders equip themselves to answer their call to do justice? The first step is to hear the call. Injustice is calling you to be a difference-maker. Climate change is alarming. Food insecurity rocks the world. Unemployment is at an all-time high. Children go to bed hungry. Poor students have no access to Wi-Fi. Rogue law enforcement officers have a plan. Marvin Gaye captured the thought in his song "Inner City Blues." Instead, answer the call. That's the second step. In other words, get involved!

## "Yes, You!": The Answer

Community engagement and social justice work are a conversion process that includes self-examination. You do well to explore questions that push you to reflect. Why is this important to me? What is at stake? What habits, outdated thinking, hurts, misinformation, and negativity need to be let go of to engage in social justice? Who is missing from your circle? What difficulties prohibit twenty-first-century thinking? Are apathy and indifference acceptable to you?

Newly married in the early 1980s, my wife and I drove to Massachusetts from New Jersey so that I could attend seminary. We had $60, a beat-up old Chevy, and a lot of faith. We never missed a meal. God paid our bills. My wife landed an excellent job. My mind was free to learn the lessons God wanted me to know for the next leg of the journey.

At Andover Newton Theological Seminary, the only two full-time Black professors took me under their wing: Eddie O'Neal and Henry Brooks. They promised me if I read the assigned books, remained open to feedback, and committed to diligent study, I would be all the better for the people waiting for me to come home to serve. Eddie O'Neal had his students read everything available on the Black church, including preaching, theology, history, administration, and leadership. Henry Brooks taught the basics of pastoral care and counseling. Brooks, along with adjunct professor and pastor O. G. Philipps, encouraged the four Black students under his mentorship at that time to take five units of clinical pastoral education and study the art of pastoral counseling. Brooks said in a lecture at the seminary on October 31, 1984, "Sometimes civil disobedience is right; but you must accept the consequences handed down by the lower authority. Count the cost." This idea was a turning point in learning a new way to be radical. Understand the human mind and use it!

Jane Carey Peck taught ethics at Andover Newton. She

exposed her students to the World Council of Churches and a few of the non-governmental organizations (NGOs) accredited by the United Nations. She offered strategies for analysis and ethical decision making. Jane Carey Peck had us read *A Theology for the Social Gospel*[3] by Walter Rauschenbusch. Equally important, she insisted on excellence and, like many professors, she was a stickler on footnotes and crediting one's sources. Peck showed us the value of well-researched activism. I drank in those lessons like cool water on a sweltering summer day. Later work with the Industrial Areas Foundation (IAF) reinforced the value added by a community organizer and advocate who employs excellent research.

Jerry Handspicker pulled it all together for me when he had us read H. Richard Niebuhr's *The Responsible Self: An Essay in Christian Moral Philosophy*.[4] Reading this text gave me a more explicit understanding of how local clergy in Rochester, New York, took on Kodak. I had my marching orders. Finally, all my experiences to date made sense. In Christian terminology, my calling was now clear. Social justice, being radical, naming the powers, and fighting Goliath were to be my life's work.

Yes, you! My education as a Freudian-trained psychoanalyst has a distinct advantage in social justice work. I grew up in Harlem, where learning how to read people accurately was a matter of life or death. Psychoanalytic training took that skill to another level. I was trained to observe body language in the same manner as FBI agents or CIA analysts. I learned valuable lessons about the human mind in four years of training while also being analyzed by one of the best, the late Sy Coopersmith.

Analysts learn how people change. Data show change occurs when people experience dramatic relief, liberation, helping relationships, understanding, hope, support, universality, information, feedback, environmental reevaluation, self-reevaluation, counterconditioning, catharsis, identification, and internalization, which means the therapy takes root.[5] Knowledge of the human mind's working allows for a deeper understanding of people's fears, anxieties, hopes, and dreams. It is also a burden. Analysists are more attuned to see the pain and hurt. More than others, we see how bankrupt systems and corporate greed injure even the strongest personalities. The insights pushed me more. Yes, you!

## Now, Go Do It—Courage

God has allowed me to be involved in seminary education for thirty-five years. I have admired the courage of colleagues who authored well-crafted statements, editorials, articles, and books. Professors have launched students to go rattle people in power. Seminary professors and administrators, like Dietrich Bonhoeffer have taken stands that put their lives and livelihoods in danger.[6] Never risk-averse, academicians have engaged in nasty confrontations with power. They did not play it safe. Yet, they were granted tenure. Trustees may have been forced to defend a radical professor who spoke truth to power. My seminary colleagues and I marched together, cried, laughed, and sent students into the world to make a difference. We instilled wisdom in our students and prayed for their courage when under fire. Seminary professors are essential! Academics are on the frontlines. They help students fine honed their courage.

Growing up in Harlem with a dad who was outspoken and a number runner afforded me a different understanding of courage and power. In my lifetime, I have received more death threats than the average clergyperson. Courage is different when a .45 Magnum is pointed in your face by an angry drug dealer. To his shock, you do not flinch, and the two of you develop mutual respect. When you are not afraid of death, you are branded either crazy or courageous.

You pick!

When God spoke to my spirit and said, "Now go do it," for me, it meant risking everything and standing up to power like Sojourner Truth, Dietrich Bonhoeffer, Martin Luther King Jr., Malcolm X, and the nuns in Guatemala, El Salvador, and Mississippi. Psychoanalysis married my call to engage in social justice with a new understanding of courage. It was clear my brand of courage was not and is not for everyone. Harlem met Freud in my training. The hard lessons learned growing up in Harlem found a home studying the human mind. My education took a revolutionary turn.

It was refreshing to understand Freud in his context. Originally, psychoanalysis was not designed for only the rich or those with health insurance. Freud ran free clinics.[7] In his private practice, about 20 percent of his patients were indigent urban residents. In Freud's era, psychoanalysts held on to the belief that a portion of their practice would go to people who could not otherwise afford treatment.[8] Additionally, Freud and his contemporaries thought it was their obligation to use their skills to help create a more just and fair society. Being a psychoanalyst is not an escape from confrontations with the abuse of power. Being a psychoanalyst helps to better equip one to address expected abuses and misuses of power!

My Harlem roots served me well when it came to work with gangs. It was clear America's focus has been on the wrong gangs. The Bloods, the Crips, MS-13, and the Latin Kings were not the most dangerous gangs in America. The gangs that scared me work on Capitol Hill. The gangs who inflict the most damage to the American people run Fortune 100 corporations. Those gangs pollute the environment, steal pension funds, contribute to global warming, promote profits over people, and create a culture of greed. Those are the gangs that scared me! Those were the gangs that God told me to confront.

The men wear white shirts and ties. The women wear

designer clothes from exclusive stores. The gang leaders are polite and professional. These gang leaders graduated from the finest schools. Their vocabulary is voluminous. But they are more vicious, vile, and vindictive than any street gang. Such gangs have been around for a long time. In fact, that was the gang that killed Jesus. That gang will kill you. Not with a gun. Instead, they use politics, policies, and laws.

Those gangs hate organizers and organized people. Like violent street gangs, the white-collar gangs make people pay the price for challenges to their power and rule. People who demonstrate a strong commitment to challenge the status quo must pay a price. There are no free lunches. Persecution, pessimism, perverted politics, and public pretenders are the order of the day. Ordinary citizens' faith is being put to the test by corrupt citizens, religious racketeers, and government greed vs. need. It is against this backdrop that God calls clergy and radicals to be courageous. Ordination is not a requirement to embrace a call to engage in social justice. But you do need courage![9]

## Why Courage?

You asked nicely. It did not work. You are in for a fight that will get nasty at times. Embrace the call and understand the consequences. Social justice is not a fight for the weak at heart or persons who cannot give and take a punch.

Courage is necessary every step of the way. Gut-check time is daily in this work. Seminaries teach a multitude of courses. The one thing seminaries can suggest but cannot teach is courage. The world does not need more timid clergy who hide at the smell of trouble. Find another line of work. Social justice work can kill you. Be clear about your level of commitment. Reflect on your strengths. God called you for a reason. Know what you bring to the table. Name your gifts. Explore with others how your gifts fit into the plan to bring about change. Discover your comfort zone. Know what makes you uncomfortable. Examine if you have the intestinal fortitude to stand up to authority. Every weapon will be used against you. Be ready. Your needs may be a hindrance or may be exploited against you and your organization. Remember, once you throw a punch, those in power will strike back. Can you spiritually, mentally, and emotionally handle a return punch? Count the cost. Where is your support, and for how long can you count on it? Clergy often discover support is inconsistent. The board that was so proud to see the pastor take a stand can turn on you. Before you win the battle, the congregation may tire of the fight. What needs does this fight fulfill for you, the congregation, and the community? Who takes care of you? How do you take care of yourself? Are you willing to take risks for the good of society? God called you. Yes, you!

## NOTES

1. Today the term is "compassionate policing." For the record, I do not support efforts to defund the police. However, I do believe budget monies can be shifted and prioritized to encourage compassionate policing.

2. My dad was a welder at both the Brooklyn Navy Yard and Hoboken Shipyard.

3. Walter Rauschenbusch, *A Theology of the Social Gospel* (New York: The MacMillan Company, 1917).

4. H. Richard Niebuhr, *The Responsible Self: An Essay in Christian Moral Philosophy*, Library of Theological Ethics edition (New York: Harper and Row, 1963; Louisville: Westminster John Knox Press, 1999).

5. J. O. Prochaska, "How do people change, and how can we change to help many more people?" in M. A. Hubble, B. L. Duncan, & S. D. Miller, eds., *The Heart and Soul of Change: What Works in Therapy*, (American Psychological Association, 1999), 227–255, https://doi.org/10.1037/11132-007, accessed March 23, 2021.

6. Eric Metaxas, *Bonhoeffer: Pastor, Martyr, Prophet, Spy*, (Nashville: Thomas Nelson, 2010).

7. Elizabeth Ann Danto, *Freud's Free Clinics: Psychoanalysis & Social Justice*, 1918–1938 (New York: Columbia University Press, 2005).

8. Patricia Gherovici and Christopher Christian, eds. *Psychoanalysis in the Barrios: Race, Class, and the Unconscious* (New York: Routledge, 2019), 4.

9. Greg Jobin-Leeds and AgitArte, *When We Fight, We Win: Twenty-First-Century Social Movements and the Activists That Are Transforming Our World* (New York: The New Press, 2016).

# CHAPTER 5

# COMPETENCE: DO YOUR HOMEWORK, LEARN, TRAIN, AND NETWORK

## Habits of the High-Tech Heart

Knowledge is power. Information literacy is a must for every radical. Persons in power fear organized people with organized money who are equipped with reasonable demands that are based on accurate research. Before you make demands, first conduct in-depth research. Know your subject matter. Like lawyers and debaters, know both sides of the argument. Be prepared for counterarguments. Do your homework! Research.

Teachers know that the world is a classroom. Every day there is a new lesson to learn. For radicals, our community is our laboratory. Technology has changed how people learn, live, and love, and the COVID-19 pandemic forced people to embrace the reality that ours is a high-tech society. Students look up and retrieve information at lightning speed. Restaurant suggestions appear on a smartphone app. Children and seniors alike play video games and electronic versions of board games. Fans order concert tickets on their laptops. Singles find love on any number of matchmaking websites. Book lovers load books by the hundreds on e-readers. Music lovers store thousands of songs on a device the size of a pack of cards. Taxpayers file their taxes electronically. Working adults program their big-screen television from the office. Photographers produce HD-quality images with smartphones, and politicians, athletes, and celebrities tweet. Welcome to the twenty-first century.

Millions write comments on social media walls. Mobile phones send real-time newsfeeds and bulletin alerts. Pet owners find lost pets in seconds with tracking collars. Automakers are manufacturing cars that drive themselves. Drones deliver packages. Movie times can be accessed on a phone. Motorists receive directions on their vehicle navigation system. Patients make appointments with healthcare practitioners in a few keystrokes. College students earn degrees without ever stepping on a campus. Worship services on streaming platforms or social media are quite common. Shoppers make purchases anywhere in the world on the internet. We live in a high-tech society.

There are advantages to living in a high-tech society, but there are cons as well. People seem to have lost touch with one another's common humanity until illness strikes. Retailers and marketers reduce people to the sum of our consumerism. Old, reliable remedies have been discarded in favor of sales statistics. Authority is measured by the bestsellers list. The world worships at the altar of a new religion: technology.

People are placing more hope in technologies than in God. Ethics have not caught up to technology. There is an abundance of information. However, our world suffers from the disease of moral malnutrition. Poor leadership has created a techno-moral crisis. Citizens do not know misinformation from disinformation. Rumor and hearsay appear in emails, texts, and blogs. Juicy sound bites have replaced responsible journalism. The pool of information grew, but knowledge declined. We know more about less. Information literacy is a must for every radical.

The internet can be your best friend or lead you down a dark path. You always must evaluate your sources. Radicals use updated technologies for research, internal communication, and social media campaigns. There are apps to keep you informed of the news, rallies, voting, causes, and much more. Technology safely used and properly vetted is a game changer. Before you go surfing the internet, consider the following themes.

## Who Do You Need to Know to Win?

Standing alone, citizens cannot win fights for justice against the powerful. Our voices are best heard and respected when we are part of a collective. Building wide networks is a valuable tool. Organizers construct power. Citizens develop the power to be heard and taken seriously through multi-faith, cross-cultural, and diverse networks working for a common cause. We stand on each other's shoulders to see further. Radicals learn from each other and from our partners.

The general rule of thumb is to meet with three people new to your circle every week. Follow up weekly with at least three current members of your circle. Should circumstances prohibit travel and face-to-face meetings, use an online platform. Administrators and corporate executives learned from their experiences during the COVID-19 pandemic that teleconference meetings save travel, reduce expenses, help people in different geographies stay connected, and are effective.

Research is more than surfing the internet. As a radical, you want to develop allies. Meet your interfaith partners. Find out who in the religious community shares your interest in social justice. Conduct one-on-ones with other faith-based

leaders. Meeting other clergy is a good starting point. Introduce yourself. Ask when you can visit. Explain you want to
get to know your colleagues. Take the stance of a learner,
scout, and trusted colleague.

Explore mutual interests. Ask what your new ally's experience with social justice is. Listen to their stories. Validate
their ministry and religious passions. Listen for common
themes. Dig without being intrusive. Always ask how you
can be of help to their work. Inquire an appropriate time for
a follow-up meeting. Be kind and supportive.

Define public relationship. You would do well to describe
your definition of a public relationship. Explain in all your
visits you are not a rubber stamp. Make it plain that you
engage in critical analysis, action, and reflection with clergy
from multiple faiths and community leaders. Be clear that
these clergy and leaders hold each other accountable for
their actions. Therefore, should your new acquaintance
partner with you in social justice work, they will also be
held responsible for their actions, policies, and practices.
Explain that relationships have points of tension: "We may
need to encourage you to listen to the people and act on a
specific issue. We have a toolkit of actions we employ to bring
attention to an issue. Our team will ask you to act. You can
expect us to evaluate your actions. We may go public with
the results of our evaluation. We can give and take a punch.
Our training is to resolve any points of tension as quickly
as possible."

Visit numerous interfaith partners. As your schedule
allows, expand your interfaith outreach. Call local religious
leaders and those within your region. Ask what faith groups
make sense for you to join. Participate in government-spon-
sored, multi-faith events. Secure a library card from the local
university and/or seminary. Make friends with the library
staff. Learn ways clergy tend to use their library. Ask the
library staff who you should add to your list to visit. Research

how clergy past and present have been involved in the region. Find out if there is a calendar of events of interest to religious leaders. Make a good lasting impression. Faith leaders can be good allies. You also want to visit community partners. Learn who operates the programs and services of interest to you and to your community. Visit the community partners that serve the members of your congregation. Discover the services and programs available in your area. Make appointments to meet various service directors and their staff. Make a list of not-for-profit organizations in your community. Assess which ones make sense to visit. Test if there is an appetite for organizing. Inquire which issues have their attention and fuel their energy. Continue to connect the dots. Investigate who is on the board of these organizations. Survey the networks connected with each program or community service. Research to discover their funding resources. Read their website and printed materials. Look for language or stances that are problematic.

Add local, county, and statewide law enforcement to your network of community partners. Meet the police commissioner, chief of police, and police captains. Discuss how to collaborate on law enforcement initiatives. Inquire what the major crimes in the area are. Learn the biggest challenges that face the department. Do your research before you meet. Go into your meetings knowing how many officers are on the force. Check the track record on minority hires and promotions. Read newspaper articles about the local and regional law enforcement. Ask how you can be of help. Learn if the department has police chaplains. What role do the chaplains play?

Should you have jails and prisons in your community, visit. Meet the warden. Know the statewide commissioner of corrections. Build relationships with multiple staff members in the prison complex. Understand the dynamics of the jail or prison. Inquire about the age of the facility, the capacity of each facility, and the current occupancy. Research what nationalities and ethnicities are represented by the correction officers.

Learn the demographics of the inmates. Know the various gangs in the facility. Be prepared by knowing which zip codes feed the prison population. Understand what educational opportunities are offered to the inmates and by whom. Be made aware of the process and cost for an inmate to see a physician. Meet the prison chaplains. Discover what is provided to meet the spiritual needs of the inmates. You are building a relationship. You always want to know how you can be of help.

You do yourself a great service to know as many judges as possible in your community and state. Members of the congregation may ask you to write a letter or appear in court on behalf of a family member. Let the judges know you. The day may come you have to write a sentence recommendation for a member of the congregation under duress. You can entertain an off-the-record conversation in private with the judge. I enjoyed being a guest host on WABC radio with Harold Goldfus, a judge in New York state. We co-hosted a lively program on Sunday afternoons in which we talked about the law as a judge and a pastor. I remember attending social gatherings in New York City filled with judges and prosecutors.

Please be sure to know your county prosecutor and staff. Meet the local sheriff. The Bergen County New Jersey Prosecutor's Office offered a series of programs for interfaith clergy when I was a pastor in that area. The one-day programs intentionally sat police chiefs next to local clergy. Participants spent the time eating, talking, and learning from each other. The prosecutor's office also invited clergy to a simulation exercise. I relentlessly teased one of the respected interfaith clergy members and a longtime friend after he shot up everybody and everything in the simulation exercise.

King's County, New York, also offered an excellent quarterly program. Interfaith clergy were invited to meet with the prosecutors, judges, and public defenders. As clergy, we heard firsthand what kind of cases were before the court. We were told of patterns of criminal activities in our community. Clergy were given a snapshot of the community through the lens of criminal prosecution and family law cases. Equally as important, we were not strangers to law enforcement and the legal system.

I found it fruitful to know federal law enforcement officials. Over the years, I have befriended members of the Federal Bureau of Investigation (FBI) and the Drug Enforcement Agency (DEA); my cousin is a retired DEA agent. It was great learning drug activity trends, user patterns, and treatment options. Such information remains quite helpful. The two agencies and interfaith partners collaborated to educate and assist the community. I was the first speaker in a seminar with the FBI to help clergy understand the law in pursuing hate crimes. We found the interaction with the FBI to be informative and helpful.

Meet the fire department leadership. Understand the causes of the fires in the community. Inquire about the morale of the firefighters. Ask how you can partner with the fire department. You may join a campaign to install smoke alarms and carbon monoxide detectors. Invite firefighters to conduct a safety check and identify opportunities to improve fire safety in your church's buildings. Bring the firefighters to discuss fire safety during worship or at a designated gathering of your choice. Inform the congregation at the holiday time of significant causes of fire. Share with your congregation how the Red Cross works with the fire department during emergencies.

Abundant Joy Community Church members found it a good practice for our church to honor the police and firefighters every year. We usually honored two police officers and two firefighters on the first Sunday of the year. Our congregation was often amazed by the stories told to us by both police officers and firefighters. I found it helpful for the police and firefighters to be formally introduced to our members. In some cases, the officers and firefighters might belong to the congregation and be known by members.

Working with political partners is necessary but can be messy for congregations. Clergy, myself included, enjoy name-dropping the governor or saying how the mayor called last night to speak about a critical issue. We feel special when high-ranking elected officials stopped by on Sunday mornings or speak at our events. We may or may not allow an elected official to speak at our worship service. Nevertheless, their presence, however real or symbolic, signals to the congregation, "We matter." I have a few friends and colleagues who had the blessing and the challenge of elected officials as members of the congregation. Under blue skies, such a relationship is excellent. But when the pastor or church opposes a position or the elected official is on the wrong side of the headlines, the skill of Harry Houdini is needed to navigate the relationship.

Radicals and clergy struggle with the place of politics in the life of a congregation. We are building power! We want relationships that represent power. Knowing elected officials is important. Over the years, I have had knock-down, drag-out fights with clergy over the place of politics in a congregation's life. From a practical viewpoint, God blesses you to expand. You need to build an education wing or build a new sanctuary. Politics are in play to gain the necessary approvals to build.

I get it; some politicians you only see at election time. Again, building for power to effect the change requires a relationship with local, regional, and federal elected officials. In some situations, it does not hurt to drop that you have a working relationship with a United States senator, a presidential cabinet member, or the president. We read examples in the Bible of men and women connected to the seats of power being able to make a difference for their people's lives. Moses, Esther, Nehemiah, Isaiah, Paul, and Jesus come to mind.

Clergy cannot underestimate the value of corporate partners. I can count more than a few times when we as ICO crashed the stockholders meeting to bring home a point. Hopefully, you have more peaceful interactions with the corporate community. I hold as a dear memory being introduced personally to the CEO and the CFO of Colgate at their annual board meeting in New York City. It is important to know the self-interests of the corporations in your region. Go far up the ladder. Sitting on local, not-for-profit boards (YWCA, United Way, Red Cross) can also serve as the gateway to meeting corporate executives.

I sat on a local, not-for-profit board. They held a statewide gathering of all the board chairs and officers for each local chapter. A quick glance of the seventy-five people in attendance identified only three people who were Black or Latinx. After two hours of stewing over it, I raised my hand. When I mentioned the lack of diversity, the director of development quickly corrected me: "We have diversity. Look around, there are Democrats and Republicans." The response reminded me of the earlier mention in the book about the blue-ribbon group working on a conference for poor people with no poor people at the table. The statewide gathering of seventy-five people discussed the not-for-profit's work in urban neighborhoods without a good representation of people from those communities.

Always be aware that your social media might be monitored by politicians, corporations, and others, especially if you sit on a board. When you post, assume it is being read by people who may or may not agree with you. They sit on a board with you. Do not be surprised by their posts on your page to downplay any expressions of anger or discord.

Black celebrities have suggested to paraphrase, "You want my body for your headcount. But you don't want me and all it means to be Black."

You have already read in this book about the value of media partners. Radicals need local, regional, and worldwide media partners. Cultivate relationships with reporters, editorial boards, and talk show hosts. You are building power. This is a give-and-take. You exchange information. Working with the media is a valuable and fruitful partnership. They can share stories, include you in articles, and point you in the right direction in your research. Having the media on your ally list is better than the alternatives.

Biblical scholars point out that the Bible records strange partnerships. Long-term organizing strategy holds there are no permanent allies or enemies; partnerships are always fluid. Support changes from issue to issue. We develop unexpected partnerships and strange allies in community organizing. Specific issues will draw the attention of persons who are allies on a specific topic. Cultivate the relationship. Remember, you may be on opposite sides on other issues. Celebrate and work together on the problems on which you agree. Learn from each other. Pay attention to how the partner gathers information. Scrutinize the information. Explore their networks. Discuss what you can learn from each to strengthen your work. Still hold to your values and principles, yet appreciate that some level of flexibility is necessary to work together. Be clear about the issue that brings you together. Agree on the level of involvement needed to put forward a united front on the subject. Exchange information. Share resources. Attend trainings. Read books and articles. If needed, explain to your base why you are part of what seems like a strange partnership. Be prepared if something in the other organization is problematic for your team.

Understand that allies are not permanent. I have lost friends over certain political or ideological stances. Everyone does not appreciate the differences between various expressions of Protestants. It does not hurt to share with interfaith colleagues how your beliefs support or challenge the issues at hand. Research the stance your faith tradition articulates on issues that matter to you. Learn how those positions may create challenges among your peers in the same faith. As stated in previous chapters, count the cost.

## What Faith-Based Texts, Practices, and Social Realities Support You?

Community engagement requires lots of collaboration. We explored context in Chapter 1. Your congregation was exegeted. We discussed how our sacred texts support social justice. Your theology was examined. Listening as a form of research has been established. You are far from finished in your preparation to be an effective change agent, however. Competence comes as you build confidence.

Two methods help increase competence. First, clergy, their congregation, and the community attend trainings and workshops that teach how to organize. Attending trainings is important. The work of relational community organizing is countercultural. You are swimming against the stream. Attending workshops is vital. You build competence by attending the trainings and applying what you learn in real situations. The workshops give you tools and principles to govern your work. Workshops offer analysis, support, networks, education, and the restoration of our humanity. Our eyes are opened. As the teenagers say, we are "woke."

Workshops, whether offered by The People's Institute for Survival and Beyond, the Industrial Areas Foundation (IAF), or other organizations, propose a paradigm shift, a new and unique way to see the world. IAF reminds its workshop attendees that there is the world as it is and the world as it ought to be. Sometimes we have been so caught up in the world as it is, we cannot wrap our head around the way the world ought to be. Workshops encourage us to see the world in a different light.

Remember, "Go do it!" Attend workshops. However, that does not conclude your learning. Practice the values, techniques, and principles you were taught in the workshops. Life after the workshop is the take-home exam. Test what you have learned. Evaluate any actions immediately to give yourself valuable feedback. How do you feel? What is your assessment of what happened in the action? What are your next steps? Who do you need to meet next? What do you think of the relationship? Was enough tension created? Maybe it was not that kind of action. Radicals do not always swing or throw punches. We can meet with powerful people to form a relationship, explore if we can be on the same page, and act as if we count on the person to answer the phone when we call.

Second, to build competence and confidence, radicals lean on our sacred texts, practices, and social realities that support us and our work. Congregations look for clear ties to sacred literature. Do the suggested practices in the workshop clash with the practices and values of your faith tradition?

The tool I developed to speak to how the community organizer training fits with spiritual practices is called the Compassion Model for Ministry. Early in my ministry, mentors told me that whatever I want to do in the congregation, hang it on Scripture. If the Bible supports your efforts, you are on solid ground. The Compassion Model for Ministry combines Scripture with practical concerns, some of which we have already covered in this book. I use the model as a checklist to ensure my desire to engage in social justice is immersed in my faith tradition's sacred literature and practices. Being a Black Baptist preacher, I stand on a history of activism. The tool is an outline filled with prompts to explore, teach, and ponder. Fit the model to your context.

# The Compassion Model for Ministry

## Ask the Right Questions

- Get the facts! Separate facts from fiction and feelings.
- What is your understanding of justice, peace, and injustices against humanity?
- What social realities bring people together or keep people apart?
- How do we find and hear the voices of "the other" and those on the margins?
- What is the "foot identification" that fosters injustice? Who is hurting? Why?
- What is your ministry? What are your available resources? What will it take to be effective?
- What does God expect of you in this time and place?
- How consistent are your espoused values, vision, and mission with your actual practice?
- What are the goals, objectives, deliverables, and outcomes? What are your priorities?
- What are your sacred texts saying to you and your community?

## Begin with a Biblical Base

- Praxis: Isaiah 61; Matthew 25:31-46; Luke 4:18-19
- Participation: Zechariah 7:9-10; Acts 6:3-7; Ephesians 4:11-12; James 2:14-15
- Power: Romans 8:26-27; 1 Corinthians 2:10; Romans 15:10
- Piety: Luke 24:49; Acts 1:12-14; Acts 1:24; Acts 2:42
- Preaching: Acts 2:14; Acts 13:42-44; Romans 10:14-17
- Priorities: Micah 6:8; Matthew 28:16-20
- Evangelism: from the Pentagon to the pew, from Wall Street to your street
- Education: protest, progress, purpose, patterns, practice, and peace

- Edification: ministry in the margins, strong in the Lord, life lit by a larger vision
- Expenditures: money for ministry, focused finances, community collaboration

## Build Relationships

- Visitation: show you care, build trust, show compassion, develop networks, affirm your worth
- Staff: surround yourself with good people, invest in their success, set the bar high
- Family: help families develop deeper intimacy, teach problem-solving, offer value clarification
- Mentor: discipleship, friendship, courtship, guidance, advocacy, teacher, consultant
- Community: capacity building, foot identification, social services, civic leaders, health, schools, business
- Power Partners: religious, political, not-for-profits, Fortune 500 companies, developers, educational

## Commit to Clear Communication

- Create clear lines of authority/accountability/responsibility. Who oversees what?
- What are the rewards and incentives? How are they communicated? Who sets the standards?
- Review: social media, websites, live streams, branding, brochures, newsletters, announcements, reports (integrity, honesty, and excitement), reputation
- Expectations: team, clergy, staff, boards, membership, community, denomination, leaders

## Keep Your Eyes On the Prize

- History: What is the history? How have others addressed this need? What is the prize?

- Values: What drives you? What are your core beliefs? What is non-negotiable?
- Mission: Why are you here? To do what or be what and for whom? How is it going?
- Context: geographic, social, economic, political, historical, spiritual, psychological
- Constitution and bylaws, federal laws, state statutes; IRS, CPA, legal team, 501(c)3

## Learn New Skills

- How do you engage in research that enables you to win over the power brokers and decision makers?
- What information outside of your congregation, community, or organization is necessary to know to support your work?
- How do you find that information?
- What skills do you need to be successful in your work?
- Where do you go for training or additional education?
- How are policies created, laws introduced, and bills passed?
- What are the engines that drive government on multiple levels?
- What research is needed to conduct effective public business on micro and macro levels?

## Seek Self-Understanding

- Limits, strengths, ability, gifts, resources, comfort zone, risks, priorities, energy
- What are we doing for the next generation? What needs does this ministry fulfill and for whom?
- How do you take care of yourself? Who mentors you? Where is the hurt/healing/help?

### Show You Care

- Show compassion, demand justice, teach mercy, embrace fairness, value integrity.
- Be biblically centered, learn their language, understand their culture, and meet their needs.
- Feed the flock through preaching, Bible study, justice ministry, and pastoral care.
- Music as ministry: compassionate therapy, a unifying force, and protest rhythms
- Celebrate prayer: Who are the prayer warriors? When do you pray? What do you pray?
- Participation: Who is at the table? Who is missing from the table? Who is calling the shots?
- Pastoral care, pastoral therapy, executive coaching, disaster preparedness, recovery work
- Diversity or managing difference: How is difference being handled? How is it recognized?

Addressing these sections over a period brings the leadership and the congregation to a deeper appreciation of how the work of social justice fits into their ministry vision. Bible studies, seminars, workshops, and preaching series have been the primary source to deliver The Compassion Model of Ministry to the congregation. I found the model to be a quick way for the congregation to dig deeper into the social realities that confront our community. I offer this to you to build competence and confidence in the work of social justice ministry.

# CHAPTER 6

# CREATIVITY: HAVE FUN WINNING BY BEING UNPREDICTABLE

## Make Your Own Rules

During the weekend of June 6-7, 2020, in Harlem and Brooklyn, New York, hundreds of Black men dressed in suits and ties led peaceful protests in response to the murder of George Floyd. The borough president, Eric Adams, led the Brooklyn protests. Signs were carried with the message "We Are Not Thugs." The traditional media were largely silent. However, pictures were blasted all over social media. Other cities have vowed to follow the lead of the Black men in Brooklyn and Harlem. This action caught the world off guard, and those of us who participated had fun doing it. That is creativity!

A march in Newark, New Jersey, drew twelve thousand participants and was hailed by MSNBC as "a model for peaceful protests."[1] Mayor Ras Baraka gave credit to the organizer of the march, Lawrence Hamm, founder of the People's Organization for Progress (POP). Baraka also applauded the police for showing restraint and the community for setting the tone for a peaceful protest. The mayor observed that people were angry, but they did not allow their feelings to turn into violence. Al Sharpton reported the story on his television program. Admittedly, I was angry that more media outlets did not report such a positive outcome with twelve thousand protestors. Such creativity and success are to be celebrated.

Some argue that there is no place for politics in the life of religious practice. It is an old argument! The argument dates to the Old Testament and continues into the New Testament. As with any argument, one can find his or her position recorded by some expert and immediately feel validated. Allow me to suggest that the Bible is filled with divine interventions and godly interactions that have political implications and radically changed human history. God urges Moses to tell Pharaoh, "Let my people go." Queen Esther approaches the king on behalf of her Jewish kin. Jesus was sentenced to capital punishment. His death led to how we mark time BC and AD.

Creativity can bump heads with traditional views of what it means to be the church. Be warned, politicians and power brokers are delighted to define the church and the personality of Jesus. Their understanding of both the church and Jesus is self-serving. For their purpose of maintaining the status quo, neither the church nor Jesus will be cast as a radical who calls the powerful into accountability and ushers in a new spirituality of inclusion and justice. Instead, politicians clumsily paraphrase from the Bible of Jesus, meek and mild. Their limited scholarship in biblical hermeneutics points to a church that is service-oriented in place of a radical activist model of spirituality. Make your own rules. The tenor of the times calls for creativity.

Radicals are engaged in an intense debate about the future of humanity. Social media and traditional communication outlets are streaming our discussion in real-time. We are drawing lines in the sand. Sides are being picked. Leaders who oppose radicals are carefully crafting position statements aimed at solidifying their base and the recruitment of new members. Their followers are poised to bring shame and sometimes even violence to any and all who disagree. The conversation has gotten heated. The stakes are high. We are talking about the future of humanity. Our concerns are both local and global. Weighing in is no longer optional; we must!

This debate about the future of humanity is not because America voted for a Black president two elections in a row. This monumental event was not triggered by the election of women as heads of state in Europe, Africa, and Asia. Please think beyond tribal conflicts, partisan politics, religious rumblings, and geographic loyalties. Climate change, the #MeToo movement, gun control, Black Lives Matter, and the personal causes of the day are symptoms of a more considerable dis-ease. The masses are yelling at tone-deaf leaders and the super wealthy that we do not like the direction humanity is headed. Your voice must be heard and taken seriously. Citizens need to engage in practical activities to make a difference in the debate about the future of humanity.

Radicals are background noise to power brokers. We must be heard! Thus, out of necessity, we must make our own rules. The power brokers' rules lock citizens out of the conversation about humanity's future. Creativity is a must for organizers.

My father preached, "Make your own rules." Strange from the lips of a former soldier. Private Will Ashley Jr. received an honorable discharge from the Army. He was laid to rest in May 1979. He died in his mid-fifties and was buried at Calverton National Cemetery in Long Island, New York.

If he were playing pool, Dad could tell you where he would place the ball with pinpoint accuracy. It was the same with baseball. On visits to Coney Island, he drew large crowds in the batter's cage. Dad would switch from playing right-handed to left-handed while the ball was thrown, and he hit it exactly where he pointed. He would suggest that the machine was broken because the fastball should not be that easy to hit. "The machine is fine, Will," my mother would say with a smile and a proud look. It was that man, my dad, who first taught me how to be radical, charming, humorous, and deadly. He also taught me to make my own rules.

My mother, Clara M. Peterkin, was 5□10□ tall and wore a size 12 dress. She was a fashion model, dress designer, beautician, and self-proclaimed tomboy. My sisters and I were told that our mom was one of the first *Ebony* magazine models. Mom was a high school graduate from Dillon, South Carolina. Like many African Americans during the 1930s and 1940s, her family of origin migrated to Philadelphia for a brief time before settling down in New York City.

Mom strongly believed in the value of two parents in the home raising kids together and she wanted that for her children. She grew up with a single mom. My grandmother and mother shared an apartment in Harlem. Living in the same apartment were my grandmother, mother, aunt, and her son. Mom was an athletic child. She loved to design dresses, and she was a wizard beautician. Like her husband, Mom lived life by the motto "Make your own rules."

According to my dad and sisters, I was a mother's boy. She taught me a quiet way to be radical. Mom was the talker in the family. Dad would just punish us and be done. Mom had to explain in detail why we were being disciplined and the consequences of such behavior once we became adults. Mom was also an excellent storyteller. She had a way with words that would leave well-respected attorneys and school principals speechless. My sisters and I watched Mom stand up to people in authority and rip holes in their arguments, which made us beam with pride.

In Mom, Dad met his match as to being fashionable. The lady could make any piece of clothing look fabulous on her model frame. Will and Clara Ashley were committed to ensuring their children received a good education, under-stood our history (family history and the Black diaspora), and enjoyed the same advantages as our middle-class white friends living on Riverside Drive in spacious apartments with a housecleaner's quarters. My sisters took ballet lessons and played their share of musical instruments. When we were not in school, it was a must that we were to be involved in some form of personal development. I played in Little League, took guitar lessons in the Carnegie Hall recital building, and housed the family library in my room.

I remember going to look for a suit for school with my dad and running into Little Anthony, a famous R&B singer. My dad said to watch how he moved about with confidence and pride. "That is how I want you to move about in the world." Meeting entertainers was not foreign to our family. Dad helped finance the first James Brown *Live at the Apollo* album with his good friend Bobby, of Bobby's Records on 125th Street in New York. The record company said, "No, we cannot see it." They thought a live album would never sell. Bobby and my dad knew better. Brown, Bobby, and my dad put their creative minds and money together to prove the record company was wrong. The lesson: make your own rules. My dad never made a dime off the sales of that album, nor did he ever receive credit for his part in the James Brown story. It was not until years later, while watching the 2014 James Brown movie *Get On Up*, that I realized the creative collaboration between James Brown, Bobby's Records, and my father.

A pattern of helping people succeed without even a thank you or any acknowledgment followed me throughout my life. Dad often said when feeding a hungry neighbor or help-ing someone navigate life's ups and downs, "Do it because it is the right thing to do. Expect nothing in return." Spouses are not always an enthusiastic fan of this way of thinking. But my mother was in full agreement.

Saul Alinsky was an expert at making up his own rules. He urged organizers to do the same. His trainings emphasized setting the table and designing the menu. To people who thought they were powerless, this was revolutionary. Organized people, with organized money, playing by their rules is a winning combination for fostering social justice.

Who said you must play by the rules? Remember, the American colonists won the Revolutionary War because their armies did not play by the standard rules of war. They caught the British soldiers off guard again and again. They changed how wars were fought. When you are outnumbered and up against more firepower, being nimble and armed with the element of surprise changes the advantage.

Global citizens stand in line to buy the next Samsung product or Apple innovation. My son and I go to the auto show every year. We want to see the creative genius of the automakers. We rush to the aftermarket section of the show, hearts pounding with anticipation to see what smart additions are available for our vehicles. Industry gets it. Innovation and creativity rock!

If you had told me when I was growing up in the 1960s that Kodak, IBM, and Polaroid would be nonexistent or fighting to make a comeback forty years later, I would have said you were crazy. As a teenager, I never dreamed an entire record collection could one day fit on a mobile telephone the size of an old cassette and smaller than an eight-track tape. Think of all the money spent on furniture to house vinyl records, cassettes, eight-tracks, VHS tapes, CDs, and DVDs. Now, thumb drives, smartphones, and the cloud hold precious pictures, degrees, and various documents. Creativity is key.

A business thrives on creativity. Read *Fortune* magazine or view the technology apps on your smartphone. New innovations, gadgets to make life easier, and apps to help with daily activities appear weekly, if not daily. The shelter-at-home orders during the COVID-19 pandemic forced people to learn the latest technology and discover the many uses of modern electronic products. Calls for creativity surround us. Imagine how effective we can be as leaders and organizers if we have a creative mindset and spirit. For the record, Jesus was creative and compassionate, yet confrontational. The three need not be exclusive of each other.

One of Saul Alinsky's principles was to have fun while fighting for justice. The action should be one that your team can enjoy. Our team of community leaders and organizers routinely give power brokers questions ahead of time for any public action. We would rather get a researched, crafted answer than "Let me get back to you. I was not prepared to address that issue." However, there are actions where our tactics call for the element of surprise or to behave differently than our standard patterns. On the positive side, we have had politicians text or call after a meeting. The text would go like this: "Great meeting. You all did not beat me up today. What happened?"

Write your script. Keep your opponent off guard. Learn how to throw curveballs and change-ups. My dad warned me growing up, "Do not be predictable. Come home a different route. Change when you leave for school or your part-time job." During a preaching course in seminary, I remember the professor urging me to "throw change-ups and curveballs in your sermons." Like a delightful story, leave the participant with, "I did not see that coming."

Let your creative side rule the day. Have fun! You are engaged in combat in every sense of the word. This is a fight. The stakes are high. It is a serious business. It is so severe that you cannot allow those against you to know your every move. What are your patterns of predictability? Learn to be proud of hearing, "We did not see that one coming."

## What Individual and Corporate Practices Foster Creativity?

Henry Mitchell and his wife, Ella Mitchell, stayed at our home when they came to preach at the church where I served as pastor, Monumental Baptist Church, Jersey City, New Jersey. Hailing from old school, their choice was staying with friends instead of in hotels whenever possible. In a dinner conversation, Henry said of himself and Ella, "We are curious as children." Somewhere between childhood and adulthood, most of us are talked out of our curiosity.[2] Artists, scientists, poets, and some preachers never give up their curiosity, and we are the better for it. Curiosity breeds innovation and creativity.

My parents fostered creativity in their three children. My youngest sister, Tina, repeatedly won the school science fair. I remember with fondness going into her room and asking, "What are you working on now?" I am also reminded of going to ask Tina if I could borrow money for a teenage date. I did not appreciate her creativity that time. Tina went in her room and returned with a sun visor on her head and bands around her arms like the old bank tellers. "Good morning, sir. The First Bank of Tina Ashley is open for business. I understand you want a loan. How do you intend to secure your loan? You understand there are interest and late fees attached. Well, sir, you qualify for a loan. Please sign this promissory note. Right now, I am not your baby sister. I am a banker. This is business." To this day, Tina is good with money.

Parents promote creativity in children. Here is what I learned from how my parents fostered creativity in their three children and my memory of what worked with my son:

1. Allow unstructured free time;
2. Discuss creativity;
3. Cultivate creative critical thinking;

4. Let kids fail; encourage them to continue to experiment and try again;

5. Encourage play outside;

6. Promote diversity in thinking;

7. Let kids pretend play;

8. Let your kids get dirty;

9. Play with your kids;

10. Teach home repairs;

11. Cook together;

12. Visit museums, zoos, parks, cultural events;

13. Ask your kids what superhero they would be and why;

14. Give your child paper and tools to draw, write, and create;

15. Help your child practice retelling family stories;

16. Praise your child; give frequent affirmation;

17. Play doctor on stuffed animals;

18. Go for discovery walks together;

19. Teach problem-solving skills;

20. Instill in your child a love for music, dance, theatre, and the arts;

21. Go to plays, operas, and concerts together; and

22. Promote learning how to play an instrument or excel in the art of telling stories through singing or as a disc jockey.

In my role as a psychoanalyst and professor, I encourage individuals and students to activate their creative side. Read and write poetry. Take a creative writing course. Learn photography, drawing, or painting. Decorate your home during holidays or during seasonal changes. Take on a home improvement project. Play word games and engage in activities that keep your mind sharp. Dress up at Halloween as your favorite character. Take music lessons, cooking classes, and courses that stretch your thinking. Learn creativity by watching your pets. Our Shih Tzu, Serafina, gives a new definition of creativity. She produces more ways to get treats, grab tissues, and get our attention. Like

Sera, permit yourself to be free, easy, and creative.

"Apple is a company synonymous with creativity."[3] The brand tagline is "Think Different." Creativity gives you a competitive edge in business. The most successful companies today are those that offer the greatest creativity. In a survey by IBM,[4] 1,500 CEOs ranked creativity as the number one factor to secure business success in the future. In a global market where everything from coffee to clothing can be purchased online, customers face multitudinous choices. Companies that foster creativity are rewarded. Customers look for the "Ah" or "Wow" factor.

How do companies encourage creativity? For starters, the companies make creativity part of the corporate culture. The office space, meeting rooms, building design, and public spaces are built to communicate that creativity is welcomed in this company. Employees are given time off to think and recharge. Downtime is not considered unproductive time. Organizers are encouraged to include downtime to think as part of our regular routine. Businesses that want creativity hire people who think creatively. They search for creative thinkers who can turn their thoughts into innovative products and services. These companies reward creativity. Companies understand everyone is not creative; however, you learn the tools and encourage such practices.

## What Is the Science Behind Creativity?

Grant Hilary Brenner authored an article in *Psychology Today*[5] asserting that the human brain operates on three different networks. There is a default mode network, the executive control network, and the salience network. According to Brenner, creativity happens when all three centers work together. Creativity is also the result of genetics and experience. Researchers discovered that creativity could also be encouraged by play, practice, and experience.

## Phyllis Harrison-Ross, MD: Creativity through the Eyes of a Black Psychiatrist

Phyllis Harrison-Ross, MD, was considered a pioneer in psychiatry.[6] She trained as both a pediatrician and psychiatrist. Dr. Phyllis Harrison-Ross trained, supervised, and mentored an army of physicians, psychologists, social workers, and hospital administrators. Written over forty years ago, her book *The Black Child*[7] is a classic on raising Black children. In her role as New York State Commissioner of Corrections under five different governors, she was a relentless advocate for inmate rights. Al Sharpton said, "I couldn't spell psychology until I met Dr. Phyllis Harrison-Ross." Sitting in a tight seat at the American Academy of Medicine on 5th Avenue in New York City, before we first met, I wondered, "Who is this lady?"

Margret Kornfeld was one of my favorite professors at the Blanton Peale Graduate Institute. She, like me, was an American Baptist clergyperson. Often, she would translate how psychoanalytic concepts are applied in pastoral ministry. Kornfeld was authoring a book, *Cultivating Wholeness*. She shared chapters with our class for feedback. It was through her kind invitation that I was in the room to hear Al Sharpton in this setting.

When the event was over, I greeted Sharpton. We were not strangers; he had preached at my church and, years ago, we had plans to partner with a media ministry. Then Kornfeld took me by the hand as we approached Phyllis Harrison-Ross. "Phyllis, how are you?" She replied with a smile, "Margret, I am doing well for an old girl. Who is this with you?" Kornfeld said, "This is my son from the Institute, Willard Ashley. He goes by Will. My son is working on a post-9/11 grant with the Red Cross and United Way. My husband and I are moving to the West Coast. Phyllis, would you take loving care of Will for me and watch over him?" I was in shock, as this was all news to me. Harrison-Ross extended her hand to me. She said, "If you care that much about him, how can I say no? Will, let us exchange phone numbers."

That was the start of a wonderful relationship that lasted until Phyllis Harrison-Ross (who self-identified as PHR) passed away January 16, 2017. We moved from mentor and mentee to friends. We became close. She summoned me during her final days on this planet and said, "When I go, you are preaching my funeral. I love Al Sharpton and Calvin Butts, but you are preaching my funeral." On Wednesday, January 25, 2017, I said words of good-bye to Phyllis Harrison-Ross, MD. My words were not adequate for such a woman, but I did my best. It was a "who's who" on the front row: former New York City mayor David Dinkins, former New York governor David Paterson, and a host of important people too many to name. You must appreciate the love and respect for PHR. The New York City police had the street blocked off at the New York Society for Ethical Culture, where she was a member. The police honor guard and bagpipe band were present at her funeral.

When I was growing up in Harlem, there was this joke that was not a joke: When the elders call, you drop what you are doing immediately and respond to their request. What was unsaid was, "Is there any part of 'now' that's difficult to understand?" The only acceptable response was and is, "I am on my way." I was reminded of this one afternoon with PHR. She called Governor David Paterson on his private phone and he did not pick up. I said, "PHR, he is the governor. He may be busy." Do you know the look an elder can give that says, "Are you that stupid or clueless?" She made another call. "Hey, it is Phyllis. I am trying to reach David." Two seconds later, the governor was on the phone, apologetic. And I mean two seconds later! PHR had called his mother. Lesson learned, when PHR says come...

Thank you to Annelle Prim, MD. She helped me to reflect on the life of PHR. When one thinks of creativity, PHR comes to mind. She is considered the mother of Black psychiatry. Celebrities proudly said in public, "PHR is my therapist." Madonna moved into PHR's co-op and did not know PHR was the president of the co-op board. She attempted to throw her celebrity weight around, which did not go well. As the kids say, "Oh, you didn't know? You better ask somebody!" Picking fights with a seasoned Black woman who is a psychiatrist is not a smart move.

PHR preached creativity and lived it. She often coached me to take the psychology stuff and add some Black Baptist preacher to it. She loved alliteration. As chair of the board at the Ethical Society Social Services Board, PHR birthed numerous innovative programs. As a New York State Commissioner of Corrections PHR was an advocate for prison reform and improvements in reentry. She was a pioneer in tele-visits for inmates to see their children and family. PHR pushed me to think creatively about my ministry, private practice, and life. I was honored that she wrote the epilogue for my book *Learning to Lead*. It was written so beautifully, and she spoke so highly of our relationship. Even today, I cannot read it without a tear. PHR was the living embodiment of creativity.

## NOTES

1. "12,000 Protesters, Zero Incidents: Newark, NJ Is a Model City for Peaceful Protests," PoliticsNation, MSNBC, June 7, 2020, https://www.msnbc.com/politicsnation/watch/12-000-protesters-zero-incidents-newark-nj-is-a-model-city-for-peaceful-protests-84631621910, accessed March 23, 2021.

2. Alison Gopnik and Tom Griffiths, "What Happens to Creativity as We Age?" *New York Times*, August 19, 2017, https://www.nytimes.com/2017/08/19/opinion/sunday/what-happens-to-creativity-as-we-age.html, accessed March 23, 2021.

3. Lauren Landry, "The Importance of Creativity in Business," Graduate Programs blog, Northeastern University, November 9, 2017, https://www.northeastern.edu/graduate/blog/creativity-importance-in-business/, accessed March 23, 2021.

4. IBM.com, "IBM 2010 Global CEO Study: Creativity Selected as

Most Crucial Factor for Future Success," https://www.ibm.com/news/ca/en/2010/05/20/v384864m81427w34.html, accessed March 23, 2021.

5. Grant Hilary Brenner, "Your Brain on Creativity: Neuroscience Reveals Creativity's 'Brainprint,'" *Psychology Today*, February 22, 2018, https://www.psychologytoday.com/us/blog/experimentations/201802/your-brain-creativity, accessed March 23, 2021.

6. Herb Boyd, "Pioneering Psychiatrist, Dr. Phyllis Harrison-Ross, Passes at 80," *New York Amsterdam News*, January 19, 2017, http://amsterdamnews.com/news/2017/jan/19/pioneering-psychiatrist-dr-phyllis-harrison-ross-p/, accessed March 23, 2021.

7. Phyllis Harrison-Ross and Barbara Wyden, *The Black Child: A Parents' Guide to Raising Happy and Health Children* (New York: Peter H. Wyden, Inc., 1973).

# CHAPTER 7

# CELEBRATION: BUILD ON YOUR WINS

Never let a victory or a defeat go by without some affirmation. Even if the action or effort goes poorly, find something to affirm and to build on for the next encounter. Celebrate your wins. Agree on what is a win. People are already beaten down. Encouragement goes a long way. Constant affirmation and acknowledgment that we are making progress are excellent recruitment tools. Like competence and commitment, celebration builds confidence. Build on your wins, no matter how large or small.

I remember the first time some seasoned leaders at Monumental Baptist Church won a victory over the mayor back in the late 1980s. They came prepared for the encounter. The leaders were armed with accurate research. Each leader had engaged in conversations with people who had the ear of the mayor. The demands were tested on the mayor's mentors and people who gave sizable contributions to the mayor's election campaign. Monumental's members and the teams from other congregations were well disciplined. Everyone knew their assigned role and stuck to it. There was not a single leader who went renegade or rogue. The laid-out plan worked to perfection. It was a moment to celebrate. The mayor agreed to place streetlights and a greater police presence on a dangerous corner near our church. He was given a timetable to complete the demand. The team showed him where in the city budget the money was available. The seed was planted for community-based police. We left food for thought: officers who know the community and are part of the community can build trusting relationships. This model is in sharp contrast to officers who live an hour's drive away and only know the community through crime statistics, emergency responses, and domestic violence calls.

Immediately after the action, we gathered on the steps of city hall and held the evaluation. The look of pride on the faces of the team was priceless. Women and men in their sixties and seventies were proud of what just happened. One woman said, "We spoke, and the mayor listened. I am just a mother and grandmother living in the projects. The mayor listened to me. So, can we go after the supermarkets that sell stale, brown meat next? I am ready." Immediately I thought, "Oh God, what did we create?" People learned their voices matter. Celebrate each victory!

We laughed. I was so happy to hear one of the seniors celebrate that her voice was heard. For the record, we did go after the supermarkets selling stale, brown meat in our community. The first victory became a confidence builder and recruitment tool. The interfaith organization began to build a reputation. Reporters began to call our leaders to weigh in on matters. Amazed citizens keep uttering, "We are being heard and taken seriously." Word made it around the congregation and community. "Who are those interfaith people?" It was a time of celebration!

At every opportunity, we held a public celebration at the church for each victory. We would insert in the bulletin copies of news articles about victories by our team. During Sunday worship, I lifted the names and accomplishments of our members who were actively engaged in social justice. We went out for meals to process and to celebrate. I wrote thank-you notes on church stationery.

Organizers are also coaches. They work on speeches and op-ed pieces, build confidence, rehearse actions, agitate, instill hope, and celebrate victories. Organizers support the masses with the reminder, "We can do this."

Barack Obama, a young senator from Illinois, took the world by storm. Ivy League-trained as a lawyer and community organizer, his message was simple yet effective: "Yes, we can." This message aligned well with his top-selling book from 2006 *The Audacity Of Hope*. Seniors stood in long lines for hours to vote. Grandmothers were in tears. People never thought the day would come when they could vote for a Black man for president. Stories of the Jim Crow south were shared with young people. Memories of the clashes and victories of the civil rights movement were alive. There was no amount of attempted voter suppression or scare tactics that would work. Ballots disappearing was not enough. America elected its first Black president.

This chapter is on celebrations. Barack Obama was creative in his campaign.[1] He openly valued small financial contributions. Every citizen felt they could contribute and make a difference. His campaign used social media in ways politics had not seen. Young people were actively involved at the highest levels. Knocking on doors was not new, but the script was new. People closed their door thinking they were being heard and respected. The message rang out loud: "I am not part of the old network. I bring fresh, novel approaches. More important, I must model civility, decorum, compassion, and competence for my two young daughters as an elected official, father, husband, and Black man." Obama's wife, Michelle Obama, would later change the world with one phrase, "They go low, we go high." Their presence as president and first lady was refreshing. In eight years, their biggest scandal was when the president wore a tan suit. Millions of Americans saw the Obama presidency as a celebration of people, from multiple cultures and varying ethnic backgrounds, working together across party lines.

My cousin Ray Chew blew the roof off as the musical director for the Democratic National Convention in 2008, the first year that Barack Obama was nominated as the Democratic candidate for president of the United States. Attendees said over and over, "Who oversees the music? Wow!" At the presidential ball, Ray was the musical director for Barack and Michelle Obama's first dance. Ray Chew became the musical director for the Macy's Thanksgiving Day Parade. Macy's had left the music in the capable hands of the same musical director for more than fifty years. Standing on his shoulders, Ray introduced fresh, creative ideas that took the music to the next level for a new generation. Over and over, I heard comments that the parade was a big celebration.

Ray, like me, learned how to celebrate from our parents and grandparents. We and our sisters gathered at Thanksgiving and Christmas with our extended family to celebrate. Between our parents and grandmothers, no expense was too big to celebrate the holidays. We spent hours cooking, decorating, playing, laughing, telling stories, and enjoying each other's company. Our first model of how to celebrate came from our family.

One of the many joys of being a pastor, professor, and psychoanalyst is the work allows me to listen to countless stories about how families from various cultures celebrate. I find it intriguing to hear the ways families celebrate milestone events such as birthdays, baptisms, anniversaries, weddings, and promotions. One of the strengths of faith-based leadership is the ability to plan and implement celebrations. The main goal in such celebrations, be they for family or in our role as a radical, is to communicate, "We care about you." Frank McMillan, the lead organizer for New Jersey Together, an affiliate of the Industrial Areas Foundation (IAF), challenged faith-based leaders in an online training December 9, 2020. To paraphrase, Frank asked the question, "Who is the leader that you would be willing to walk through a wall or die for?" His question seared my soul. I wondered how many people, if any, in my congregation or classes would have responded to that question with my name. Frank shared persons who fit that bill have a few common characteristics. The three that stuck out in my mind were: (1) They care about you without an agenda other than your well-being, (2) They care about what you care about, and (3) Such souls care about people regardless of their politics, ideologies, religious practices, and demographics. Sounds to me like the characteristics of a healthy family. Our celebrations ought to communicate all that Frank called to our attention in the training.

Celebrations were a big part of my family. Family life strikes a sentimental chord in me. Faith-based leaders can find strength and the much-needed support in family life. We are first taught the value of relationships and celebrations by our families. Congregations and not-for-profits can be and are an extension of family caregiving through celebrations.

Jesus saves lives! Give me those old-fashioned family values any day. Real truths have been replaced with cyber-babel. People settle for information without intimacy. We want success, sex, and stuff without restraints. Celebrations must be fun. However, celebrations should not lead to regrets. Our parents and grand-parents taught us to celebrate responsibility.

Political figures celebrate after an election victory. The acceptance speeches are filled with hope for a better future. Each speech is infused with the promise of a new day. New opportunities are painted as the standard for their administration.[2] The party atmo-sphere is a reminder that volunteers and paid staffers believed in the candidate and supported his or her vision for a better tomorrow. The slogans and campaign ads say, "I have a better plan; let us celebrate success together."

Any sports fan sees how their favorite athletes celebrate. Race car drivers down milk. Champagne flows in the club house after the Super Bowl is won, NBA champs are crowned, World Series pennants are won, and the Stanley Cup is secured. Huge cigars come out, and the commercial "I just won the Super Bowl. I am going to Disney" plays on television. Fans enjoy the celebrations after a football touchdown. Baseball purists argue that there is no room for big celebrations after home runs. But baseball players do congratulate and express their joy after a home run with one another on a smaller scale. My lifelong favorite baseball team, the New York Yankees, has all the players who were on base meet at home plate to congratulate the player who hit the home run. Professional golfers celebrate after a tournament win. Boxers do a victory dance after a fight win. Soccer players run the field after a score. Hockey players hug and do the one-leg fist pump. Who doesn't get excited when the puck goes in the net, the announcer echoes, "Score!" and the siren goes off? Sports figures and teams celebrate.

Mass movements celebrate. Wyatt Tee Walker once told me on a long international flight that the celebration is part of the action in organizing. You fight hard against injustice. You fight hours and minutes before big rallies and major speeches. Wyatt, who was Martin Luther King Jr.'s chief of staff, shared how many knock-down fights the brain trust had leading up to some of King's most famous historical moments. After such tension, you need to exhale, let off steam.

Victories are celebrated in many ways in mass movements. Recognition is first given in written notes, email, texts, announcements, articles, press releases, and news conferences. Media presence ads to the celebration to record and report the joy of a hard-fought victory. If there is extra budget money, parties and vacations are welcomed if it fits the movement's ethics and bylaws. Congregations and organizations give plaques, award banquets, proclamations from elected officials, and affirmations posted on social media or news apps.

It always warmed my heart to read articles in the media that outlined ICO, Jersey City Together, and New Jersey Together victories. After a thirty-year fight to clean up chromium from the west side of Jersey City and build affordable housing, it was a joy to hear Mayor Fulop and others acknowledge our work. Our organizer, Frank McMillan, sent me the press release. Joe Morris, who walked with ICO for years as our lead organizer on this fight, sent an email of congratulations. Our team sent congratulatory notes to each other. On our video call due to COVID-19, I could see the big smile on Father Geoff Curtiss's face. "Will, how hard can it be?" Not hard, Geoff, just thirty years. Thank you!

## How Racism Changes the Celebration

During our celebrations about affordable housing, racism changed the topic. Widespread abuses by police, even as the world was watching, left us totally baffled. Racism is a cancer that kills celebrations, dreams, and our shared humanity. What is needed to celebrate the end of racism? Can the energy of the summer of 2020 be sustained to move to a new push to change laws, policies, practices, and racist systems? Are white people willing to let go of privilege, historic realities, and not-so-hidden biases to form partnerships of mutual respect and accountability with Black people and other persons of color? Can we change "We Shall Overcome" to we have overcome? Claud Anderson wrote,

> It is now time for Black people to create wealth for themselves. The secret to creating wealth is to own and control resources, whether they are natural (land, water, precious minerals and metals), processed (machinery, factories, consumer items, public improvements), or human capital (skilled, literate, labor force). The late Carl Bell suggested that Black psychiatrists need not find new ways to treat rat bites; but eliminate the rats.[3][4]

Before there was a T.D. Jakes or a Joel Osteen, Adam Clayton Powell had fourteen thousand members in his congregation in 1945. Powell said there is no separation of church and state in the Black church. The 501(c)3 was designed to give money to those in need. One can argue the backroom stories and justification for the laws to govern the 501 (c)3.[5]

Read your history. It is always about race, sex, power, and

the distribution of resources. Politics, police, and the church are tasked with keeping the law. Asking people to think differently is countercultural. But we must. You want to celebrate. Change the wealth gap. America was built on the backs of Black slaves, followed by poorly paid workers.

What do Black people own? What owns Black people? What do Black people need to be independent, free, wealthy men and women? Al Sharpton preached at George Floyd's funeral, "Get your knee off our necks."[6]

## Get Your Knee Off Our Necks

In 2019 the combined buying power of African Americans, Asian Americans, and Native Americans was estimated at $2.4 trillion. In 2018 Black buying power, according to Nielsen, was at $1.2 trillion.[7] The top expenditures were housing, food, cars, clothing, and health care. Some educators assert third-grade reading scores are predictors of the likelihood that one may become an inmate.[8] Studies show many Black males mentally drop out of school at the age of nine and await the legal age to leave physically. Prisons are being built across the street from run-down high schools in urban centers. Bill Gates and Jeff Bezos have more net worth than all Blacks in America. Multiple sources report the median wealth of Black Americans may fall to zero by 2053,[9] and that was before the COVID-19 pandemic! Blacks have had trouble creating wealth in America. Nikole Hannah-Jones asserts it is not the result of some character flaw, lack of education, or an unwillingness to work hard. The core of the problem is a systemic, willful strategy to keep Blacks from wealth creation.[10] Black males are four times more likely than white males to be suspended or expelled from school.[11] Blacks who get by pay a tariff for the privilege of driving while Black. Try to hail a cab. Park your Mercedes in an elite mall. You want to celebrate. Undo racism. Get your knee off our necks. Then we can celebrate together.

Read Claud Anderson. Listen to his lectures. Visit his Black think tank. He lifts three major impediments that stop celebration in Black America. The first impediment is the maldistribution of wealth and resources. Name a Black-owned hotel, airline, or fast-food chain. Take your time, I will wait. Go into any mall in America; how many of the chain stores are Black-owned? How many professional sports teams are owned by Black people? Other than Byron Allen, how many Black people own cable networks, major television stations, or media outlets? In the 1990s and at the turn of the century, I attended a few lectures by Claud Anderson in churches and civic venues. He repeated in each lecture, "We are players in a real live Monopoly game. Whites own the board and all the pieces on the board." Anderson was referring to how white developers, banks, real estate agents, and government agencies hold the seats of power and handle neighborhoods as if playing a game of Monopoly or chess.

Why are people poor? What keeps poor people poor? Who owns the means of production? Racial prejudice and power impose their way of life. Systemic racism is a social contract based on race. Racism is a wealth- and power-based competitive relationship between Blacks and whites. The sole purpose of racism is to ensure the white majority uses Black labor to create wealth. Racism is a multigenerational process of disempowerment. Racism is not natural; it is a learned behavior. Blacks ask institutions (banks, schools, government) to do what they were not designed to do for African Americans. The People's Institute for Survival and Beyond says in its workshops that Blacks cannot be racists because we lack the wealth, power, or control to marginalize the white race. Black people can think bigoted thoughts, but we lack the power to impose our thoughts on white people. And the few that do are demonized and destroyed.

The second impediment to celebration in Black America is inappropriate behavior patterns. People of the African diaspora in America suffer from internalized racial oppression. White people see me as invisible in meetings, malls, at work unless I appear dangerous. Then they call the police. I am 6'2" and about 230 pounds, 210 pounds in my slim days. Can I tell you how many times I have been the next in line to be served at a store, post office, or restaurant, and a white person has walked in front of me as if I was not standing there? Every time I have asked the question, "Did you see I am next in line?" I have been met with, "Oh, I did not see you standing there." And my internist tells me to reduce my stress! "Since you do not see me then, you will have to see me now." Notice Black dress norms, behavior in public places, and conspicuous consumption. We are saying, "Can you see me now?"

Internalized feelings of racial inferiority are found in thinking the white man's ice is colder than the Black woman's ice down the street, or the white man's watermelon is sweeter than the brother's watermelon on the truck in the hood. There are Blacks who do not want to be Black. They adopt white European culture and thinking wholesale. But, get into trouble, they call Reverend Al Sharpton or the NAACP. It has been my experience over a span of fifty years that there are educated Blacks who uncritically buy into terms like diversity, people of color, and minority, not realizing those terms were designed to dilute Black power and wealth.

The internalized racial superiority of white people adds to the problem. White privilege and entitlements. Thinking it is okay to be clueless about other cultures or that Blacks protect white folks. White people are quick to point out self-destructive behavior among African Americans. Black pain is exploited when white "experts" know more about racism (at a few thousand dollars a lecture) than people of the African diaspora.[12] The media support exaggerated visibility. Burger King News: Have it your way. Blacks are the problem! They need to be controlled and supervised.

How can we celebrate? What can we do to end racism? The easy answer is organizing. The devil is in the details. I pray that you sign up to participate in the "Undoing Racism" workshops. You need basic training, a common analysis, a shared language, and mutual support. Anything you read in this book is not a substitute for attending the workshops offered by any colleagues and their organizations. Be it online or in person, attend the workshops, trainings, and lectures. Claud Anderson is right: we need a national plan. The Poor People's March is one, but there are others. Remember creativity. Right now, Black people lack a national strategy to undo racism. And that is fine with white supremacists and power brokers. Their motto: Stay broke and un-woke! Black leaders keep treating rat bites instead of eliminating rats. Gatekeepers continue to translate people's reality into language approved by the power in exchange for resources. Mention race or racism without approval and your show is canceled, off the air. Publishers soften the blow of racism so as not to offend their white customers. What is needed is a code of conduct (Ma'at[13]); group accountability, and an independent economy (okay, I am in trouble now).

Black people confuse wealth with income. Chris Rock got it right. Basketball and football players have income. Jerry Jones, the Dolans, and the Steinbrenner family have wealth. They can decide not to let someone play in our area or stadium. They can trade a Black player or just cut them from the team. They have the power. Let us organize to expand the churches' role to teach a new focus around Blacks as the original people. Can the public schools teach honest and accurate history? Churches can develop and instill a group code of conduct that promotes social cohesiveness, values, and norms (like the Deacons for Defense and Justice[14] or the Nation of Islam). All the congregations that called me as the senior pastor had armed security (usually off-duty officers, federal agents, or uniformed local police). This is a common practice among faith-based institutions. Churches can teach Black economic prosperity and operate the church as an educational center.

Push for expanded reading lists to include Black history. Hold seminaries and universities accountable to teach Black perspectives and encourage Black scholarship that is not dependent on white, European values and perspectives. Grant tenure to professors who take a public stand against racism and who publish articles read by the masses to offer tools and encouragement. For every Cornel West, Kimberlé W. Crenshaw, and Eddie S. Glaude Jr., there are hundreds of Black faculty members who are denied tenure because, off-record, they were too radical, too Black. Kenneth V. Hardy asserts in his workshops, lectures, and written materials that graduate schools teach minorities how to be a GEMM (good, effective mainstream minority).[15] As such, our training is Euro-centered. Rarely if ever does our education include multicultural perspectives or scholarship that does not have dominant culture, white supremacist roots. GEMMs are rewarded when we stay in our lane, do not rock the boat, and know how to behave in such a matter that does not scare white people. We do not discuss race. GEMMs maintain our invisibility without complaint. Minorities play the GEMM game to get ahead. I was no exception. Being a GEMM is how I was granted tenure and became the first Black dean of the seminary. One can express only so much anger and rage as a GEMM without consequence.

Get your knee off our neck. Then Black people can celebrate with white people as equals in the experiment called America.

## NOTES

1. Andrew Boyd, *Beautiful Trouble: A Toolbox for Revolution* (New York: OR Books, 2016), 234.

2. Ezra Klein, *Why We're Polarized* (New York: Avid Readers Press, 2020), 17–20.

3. Claud Anderson, *PowerNomics: The National Plan to Empower Black America* (Bethesda, MD: PowerNomics Corporation of America, 2001), 121.

4. David Kopacy, "Carl Bell, MD: Medical Activist & Human Rights Champion with an Indomitable Fighting Spirit," Being Fully Human, July 18, 2020, https://beingfullyhuman.com/2020/07/18/carl-bell-md-medical-activist-human-rights-champion-with-an-indomitable-fighting-spirit/, accessed February 15, 2021.

5. Paul Arnsberger, Melissa Ludlum, Margaret Riley, and Mark Stanton, "A History of the Tax-Exempt Sector: An SOI Perspective," *Statistics on Income Bulletin*, Winter 2008, https://causeinspiredmedia.com/

wp-content/uploads/2017/02/tehistory.pdf, accessed February 15, 2021.

6. George Floyd Eulogy, June 4, 2020, https://youtu.be/CGVN5F_BQK0.

7. Ellen McGirt, "raceAhead: New Nielsen Report Puts Black Buying Power at $1.2 Trillion," *Fortune*, February 28, 2017, https://fortune.com/2018/02/28/raceahead-nielsen-report-black-buying-power/, accessed March 23, 2021.

8. Troyatmls, "The Relationship Between Incarceration and Low Literacy," The Official Blog of Literacy Mid-South, March 16, 2016, https://literacymidsouth.wordpress.com/2016/03/16/incarceration-and-low-literacy/, accessed February 15, 2021.

9. Charlene Rhinehart, "African American Wealth May Fall to Zero by 2053," *Black Enterprise*, July 12, 2019, https://www.blackenterprise.com/african-american-wealth-zero-2053/, accessed March 23, 2021.

10. Nikole Hannah-Jones, "What Is Owed," *The New York Times Magazine*, June 30, 2020, https://www.nytimes.com/interactive/2020/06/24/magazine/reparations-slavery.html, accessed March 23, 2021.

11. Matthew Lynch, "Black Boys in Crisis: Eliminating the School-To-Prison Pipeline," The Edvocate, September 21, 2017, https://www.theedadvocate.org/black-boys-crisis-eliminating-school-prison-pipeline/, accessed March 23, 2021.

12. Courtland Milloy, "Black Psychiatrists Are Few. They've Never Been More Needed," *The Washington Post*, August 11, 2020, https://www.washingtonpost.com/local/black-psychiatrists-are-few-theyve-never-been-more-needed/2020/08/11/7df9eeea-dbeb-11ea-8051-d5f887d73381_story.html, accessed February 6, 2021.

13. Ma'at was an ancient Egyptian code of conduct and principles by which to live. The Africentric Eye, The Principles of Ma'at, http://theace.me/maat-principles.html, accessed February 6, 2021.

14. Black war veterans united to protect civil rights groups from the KKK and other white supremacists. Elwood Watson, "Deacons for Defense and Justice," Black Past, November 19, 2007, https://www.blackpast.org/african-american-history/deacons-defense-and-justice/, accessed February 6, 2021.

15. Kenneth V. Hardy, "On Becoming a GEMM Therapist: Work Harder, Be Smarter and Never Discuss Race," in *Revisioning Family Therapy*, 2nd ed., Monica McGoldrick and Kenneth V. Hardy, eds. (New York: The Guilford Press, 2008), 461–468.

# CHAPTER 8

# CHARACTER:
# THE WAR HAS JUST BEGUN

## Leadership Opportunities and Obstacles for Faith-Based Leaders

While you celebrate victory, your opponent is not taking defeat lying down. Expect a reaction. ICO had encounters with elected officials whereby as we were leaving their office, persons with opposing views were in the waiting room to see that official next. We were not shocked when, after speaking with the opposition (usually big business, developers, or financial institutions), the elected official a few times reversed or revised his or her agreement with our team. Remember, most times, power brokers are happy with the status quo. The fight is to be heard, be taken seriously, and have our professionally researched, reasonable demands met. Any reason to keep things as they are will be used. It is what I call the dark side of leadership.

Character is built on how you handle the critique, attacks, and attempts to dilute your power. People in power are not used to losing and do not expect to lose the next time.

Understand that one victory does not end the conflict. The war has just begun. What are common attacks to expect? How do people handle the attacks? What positive character traits will sustain you during the long haul? What if the fight takes decades? How do you keep the faith and maintain your hope? How can you remain consistent during the rollercoaster of fighting for justice? What is the role of family and mentors to keep you grounded? You won your first victory. Now the war has just begun. Allow me to address these questions in the next few pages of this closing chapter. Remember, the ICO fight to clean toxic waste to build affordable housing took thirty years. How do you maintain momentum and sustain the fight when the end seems distant?

I first shared the Dark Side of Leadership model outside the classroom at the General Baptist Convention, New Jersey, under the leadership of Dr. Lester Taylor, during their Congress of Christian Education in April 2017. The model was fine-tuned when I remarried. My wife, Tanya Pagan Raggio-Ashley, who trained at Rutgers Medical School, offered a physician's perspective and the touch of a Latina from the Bronx.

## The Glamorous Side of Leadership

Let us be brutally honest. There is a glamorous side to leadership. Being a rabbi, imam, priest, or pastor has some benefits. Our position is respected and revered most of the time. People respect the position. Even those who wish we would resign respect the position. Certain establishments offer clergy discounts. We go on paid vacations because a cruise line asks a clergyperson to conduct morning worship services and answer spiritual or religious questions from the passengers. If our tradition allows married clergy, people ask their spouse, "What is it like being married to a pastor (or rabbi, or imam)?" Dating is much more of a challenge for single clergy because of our position and the expectations placed upon us.

Clergy have a degree of power. If nothing else, we decide which sacred texts to preach and teach. If we work from a lectionary, we can hear God speak to us on how to handle the text for our listeners. Black pastors, megachurch clergy, and Catholic priests tend to have more power within the congregation. Younger clergy do not fully appreciate that such power is earned. It comes with walking with people during challenging times in life. Power in the church is the result of a track record of good decisions and appropriate behavior. Power is given to us by God. Having trusting, respectful relationships in the congregation affirms that power. If power is abused, it is lost. Numerous biblical examples confirm my statement.

One of the glamorous sides of leadership is our piety. People are in awe of religious leaders' spirituality and religiosity. We are experts and students of our sacred literature. Our messages heal hurts and confront the comfortably complicit. Clergy visit people in the hospital and lift spirits of broken bodies. We are asked to pray before surgeries. Clergy are asked to offer the invocation in the halls of power. We read Scripture at the bedside before life-altering events. Stories of our piety stretch far and wide. "I was feeling down. Pastor prayed for me and the burden lifted." It is quite common to hear a testimony of that sort.

In my own ministry, I have been amazed at the ability to touch people and hear their medical reports confirmed they were healed. I do not claim to be a faith healer. It is not a gift that works with the camera rolling on cue. However, the ten or so times God used my hands to heal, the person on the other end shared the news with me. I remember being mad at God. One of my biggest thorns in the congregation thanked me for healing her body and then continued her attacks on me at every opportunity. Our positions come with a certain respect for our piety. We bless marriages at receptions after we performed the wedding. We baptize. We talk to God.

Clergy have a level of prestige. Clergy wear symbols of our position: a collar, cross, or stole. We receive immediate reactions. People refer to us by our title out of respect. In some faith practices, you are called by your first name, but your title is attached. "Hey, Pastor Glenn!" Elected officials, media, corporate entities, medical personnel, celebrities, you name it, know us not by our names but as Reverend, Pastor, Rabbi, Imam, and Priest. We attend events and people announce, "Reverend is here." Clergy are offered seats of honor at events. Conversations change because we are present.

Lastly on the glamorous side are the politicians. We are invited for photo opportunities with elected officials. I cherish that I can text an elected official or have them come by to say hello to the congregation. We are close to the seat of power. Their staff knows us. Specific changes to the fabric of the neighborhood are made because we asked an elected official. Jobs are secured for us, a family member, or a congregant. The clergy feel special when an elected official calls our name at an event. One of my professors, who taught a course on persuasion at Montclair State University, called this "association with greatness."

## The Dark Side of Leadership

"We have this treasure in earthen vessels" (2 Corinthians 4:7, KJV). The late William A. Jones Jr. said, "There is treasure in the trash." A quote sometimes attributed to Shakespeare states, "A friend is one that knows you as you are, understands where you have been, accepts what you have become, and still gently allows you to grow." Clergy need friends and colleagues who accept us as we are warts, and all. Such friends and colleagues see our shadow side, pray, and coach us toward growth. Those are souls who do not exploit our failures and shortcomings.

There is a dark side to leadership. Rest assured your enemies, haters, the status quo protectors, and others will exploit your dark side. It has always amazed me how people are quick to identify leaders by our illnesses, shortcomings, mistakes, or sins. Sitting on the abysmal edge of this reality we call life, God called us to lead, but it costs us.

## Pragmatic Pitfalls

The late Gregg Mast was the president of the New Brunswick Theological Seminary. During the five years that I served as his dean of the seminary, we interviewed people for various positions. Gregg would ask at the end of each interview, "What keeps you up at night?" Upon Gregg's retirement, the new president wanted a new dean to carry his vision. Gregg called to check how I was handling the transition. We spoke and laughed like old times. As the conversation ended, Gregg said, "Will, deans are up at 2:00 a.m. sending emails to the president or watching the news to confirm if we close the seminary due to weather. In your new role, you can sleep through the night." Gregg died due to complications from COVID-19. Before his untimely death, Gregg revealed he kept on his desk the signed baseball I presented to him at his retirement dinner. The baseball was signed by Mariano Rivera of the New York Yankees. Rivera was a closer and one of, if not the, best reliever in the history of baseball and saved countless games for his team. Gregg often said that, like Rivera, we saved an institution on life support with a storied history. We closed the deal that restored the finances of New Brunswick Theological Seminary and built a new thirty-thousand-square-foot main building.

Four things keep clergy up at night: budgets, buildings, blueprints, and butts. We worry about the finances of the church. The worst church fights are usually not over theology or biblical literacy but the budget and finances. Giving is down; preach tithing. How abundantly are we blessing the pastor? How much does the music department cost the church? Why are we on television and radio? We need money for a new roof. The building needs a paint job or to be steam-cleaned.

Snow days, sheltering at home due to COVID-19, and any closure of the building has a direct impact on giving. Meeting payroll and ensuring there is adequate money to fund the church's vision is stressful. Clergy were forced to make some tough financial decisions during the COVID-19 pandemic. My heart went out to the clergy with huge mortgages to pay. Buildings keep clergy up at night. Some of these older, beautiful buildings are monsters to maintain. Stained-glass windows are lovely to view, but I know firsthand they are expensive to maintain. The slate roofs, old boilers, and noisy radiators are just a few of the expensive items to upkeep. Buildings and budgets are pragmatic pitfalls. Politicians can use them against you. "Reverend, if you run a daycare center at your church, it solves your financial problems." Of course, there are always strings attached, like buying your silence on certain issues.

God blesses us. We start a building program or Christian Education building or expand our campus. Most of us did not take seminary courses to know about zoning laws, codes, and blueprints. We must trust our lay leaders and forepersons to oversee the project on our behalf. Mentors have told me that building projects and blueprints kill pastors.

Clergy are concerned about butts in the seats or on the live stream. We equate membership with power. That is not always the case. A small congregation can be well organized, with people in power or who have access to power among the members. With new realities upon us, how houses of worship place butts in the seats will be of concern. Clergy struggle with pragmatic pitfalls.

## Persistent Pressures

The dark side of leadership burdens clergy with persistent pressures. Over the years I have identified three: the failure of science; the frustration of suffering; and the fatigue of shame. Clergy are the ones responsible for healing individuals and families when science fails. COVID-19 is a prime example. Clergy were on the frontlines to ensure, even during a pandemic with no cure in sight, people were provided hope. The physician walks out after delivering unwelcome news and the clergyperson steps in to help the patient cope. We are expected to offer comfort, and we struggle when there are no easy answers for the failure of the science. We permit patients and families to look up to God and scream, "Why?"

Every person privately struggles with the frustration of suffering. We watch beloved members die. People have unexpected accidents and leave this world. Cancer strikes a beloved member, and they endure a slow death. We are exposed to people who were once so full of energy but have now given up as their body suffers. We pray. God does not give the answer we want. We see racism rip out the hearts of people. We are frustrated that others do not see what we observe.

We live in a shame-based society. Others enjoy our moments of shame. We grow weary hearing about the shame heaped on others and acknowledging that if our secrets were revealed, we too would feel the impact of shame. Law enforcement, politicians, prosecutors, trial lawyers, and our haters work to expose our shameful moments. During my seminary days in the 1980s and 1990s, Henry Brooks was the chair of the psychology department at the Andover Newton Theological School. He shared in the introduction to pastoral care course not to run from your shame; own it. Yes, I am that, but it does not negate the fact that your product poisons people. In other words, do not allow your human failures to be used against you to quiet the demand for justice.

Know that as others attempt to shame you and use your past or present to silence your witness against injustice, you are in good company. Noah had a drinking problem (Genesis 9:20-21). Moses flunked anger management (Numbers 20:10-12). Elijah was depressed (1 Kings 19:4-14). David committed adultery (2 Samuel 11:1-5). Solomon was a womanizer (1 Kings 11:1-5). Jeremiah kept crying (Jeremiah 13:17). Hosea married a prostitute (Hosea 1:2). Peter denied Jesus (Luke 22:54-62). Judas was a thief (John 12:6). Jesus was convicted (John 19:1-16). John saw things (Revelation 4:1-11).

Your shame is ever before you, but keep on protesting, organizing, and serving. God does not call perfect people to serve as religious leaders.

### Private Prayers

Clergy pray three private prayers: the worry prayer—forgive me, I have sinned; the wounded prayer—free me, I am suffering; and the weary prayer—fix me, I am sick. Psychologically you stayed a victim, sank into the valley, and are seeking the victory! These are the secrets and shame that others who oppose social justice will gladly share to discredit your campaign. Talk radio shows will lift up a bad example for the cause: "Wasn't that the guy who was busted with coke in his car?" Again, it does not mean you got the justice issue wrong. It can and will be used as a tactic to attempt to silence you and discredit your organization. Grow tough skin. If you are guilty, pay the consequences and keep fighting for justice.

### Painful Predicaments

What trips clergy up are sin, scandal, secrets, shame, sickness, suffering, separations, and strife. People who hold public office are admittedly guilty of one or more of these challenges. People in power can forgive and forget what serves their agenda. It is mind-blowing to play back conversations and observe how politicians and some preachers can do an about-face when their person is caught on the wrong side of a scandal, sin, secret, or shame. Again, the exposure is not because they care about you and want to help you recover. The goal is to eliminate you from the public.

**Problematic Practices**

Okay, it is not scandal, sin or shame that is wearing you out. You have trouble with fitness, food, faith, family, friends, and finances. Any one of these can be a problem. Clergy are under tremendous stress. Among the duties of clergy are meeting deadlines for sermons, eulogies, board meetings, community engagement, hospital visits, and at times watching beloved members die. Disasters both natural and human created along with a worldwide pandemic put clergy at risk for burnout, depression, high anxiety, and self-defeating behaviors. For decades, I have conducted wellness seminars for clergy on what I call the Stressful Six, fitness, food, faith, family, friends, and finances. The Stressful Six are the personal challenges clergy face in addition to the ones related to the vocation of faith-based leadership.

It is important that clergy attend to self-care. Best practices include regular exercise, proper nutrition, hydration, sleep, career satisfaction, spiritual disciplines, and other lifesaving activities outlined later in this chapter. Faith-based leaders can be their own worst enemy when any one of the Stressful Six is out of balance or neglected.

## Strategies that Lead to Healthy Leadership

How do you keep your body, mind, and spirit in decent shape for the long haul? What is the secret to staying healthy in a highly stressful career and ministry? On a clergy support call when I said, "Undoing racism is a long-term marathon," one participant responded immediately, "How do you sustain your energy and health for the long term?" My response was, "Great question. Can I share what I learned during a thirty-year fight for justice in Jersey City?" The group of twenty-five organizers was left hanging until the next meeting. However, let me share with you my secret right now. These are the five activities to get you through long-term organizing efforts.

### Learn Your System

Conduct a "foot analysis." As Ron Chisom of The People's Institute says, "Identify the foot that is kicking your butt." Explore what the challenges in your leadership are. Back to Gregg Mast, "What keeps you up at night?" What threatens your ministry?

1. shackled by the board,
2. sex,
3. money,
4. power,
5. ministry in the margins,
6. loneliness,
7. the thrill is gone,
8. job satisfaction,
9. who is in charge,
10. part-time pay, full-time work,
11. pay a pastor or fix the boiler,
12. utility bills,
13. repair the roof,
14. where is the crowd,
15. family,
16. bitter, better or blessed

Find a good therapist to help you process what is out of balance in your life. How healthy are you? Who helps the helper? What kind of help do you need? How is your love life? How is your attitude? Sick leaders lead sick institutions! Get help. Health is contagious. Remember, followers usually want to please the leader. Typically, only a handful fight and rebel. Do not allow the small minority to rent space in your head for free. Be confident. Let the attacks build character.

## Look at Your Stressors

What does it mean to be Christian? How you answer the question will dictate your piety and inform your practices. The answers can stress you. How do you seek justice? How can you make a difference? How did God single you out for significance? Where does one go to learn how to be holy? Is holiness reserved only for Catholics, Pentecostals, and evangelicals, or is holiness a requirement for all Christians? Is there room for holiness in the business of the church? If so, how is holiness manifested when one's faith, finances, and future are under fire? Feeling stressed?

See your healthcare provider once a quarter. It is worth the visit. If you have health challenges, explore those with your healthcare team. You want to check out your physical health. I go for my annual checkup once a year. My dermatologist conducts a full body scan once a year to check for unusual lumps, spots, or skin issues. I see various specialists about two to three times a year for check-in. During the pandemic, my health team checked on me via telemedicine. You should monitor your energy, fitness, and overall wellness. Your goal is prevention. Self-monitoring is essential. What are you trying to check?

COVID-19 presented an additional list of stressors and opportunities for faith-based leaders. During the pandemic, faith-based leaders were deemed essential even without that declaration by governments and emergency administrators. We offered society hope, strength, and an anchor during uncertain times. We were the calm steady voice in the midst of the triple pandemics of COVID-19, systemic racism, and petty politics. Ours was and remains the task of accurately separating facts from fiction and falsehoods. Faith-based leaders accepted the task to forge faith from fears. We challenged ourselves to be less bureaucratic and more relational. We made daily and weekly phone calls to check on our congregational members. I heard stories from clergy and their congregations how great it felt to receive constant check-in calls. Hundreds of people shared with me the joy of feeling that their faith-based leader actually cared about them as a person instead of as an offering envelope number or a ministry chair. Pastors, priests, rabbis, and imams were reminded during this pandemic of the power of relationships. The theme was loud and clear: We need to pray for each other as Hezekiah Walker sings about in his song "I Need You to Survive."

Ministry is contextual. Everyone was not in the same place during the pandemic. Each soul experienced different degrees of stress. The realities of contextual ministry created greater stressors on some faith-based leaders than others. Radicals are called to address an injustice, disaster, pandemic, or crisis through three lenses: personal, professional, and prophetic. Faith-based leaders are not some clean slate without personal attachments, feelings, or challenges of our own. The pandemic tested our courage, resolve, and health. We were not the experts flown into a situation to bring healing and leave. We lived the drama, horrors, and questions every day, either from a safe distance on our screen or on the frontline of the battlefield. We lost colleagues in ministry. Some faith-based leaders were stricken with disease or their preexisting conditions acted up. Like me, many faith-based leaders were worried about their families. This pandemic was personal. The added stress this pandemic caused was real.

Following the tragedies of 9/11, Hurricane Katrina, the COVID-19 pandemic and other natural and human-made disasters, professional and lay faith-based leaders reported feeling overly tired. These intimate moments of reflective sharing came during the numerous clergy support groups I led. Some felt they were carrying a multitude of emotions on a rollercoaster ride. In addition to our personal challenges, clergy, clinicians, and caregivers took on professional stressors. Our calling during the COVID-19 pandemic was video hospital visits, shortened funerals, drive-by communion, unique worship services online, live-stream preaching to empty pews, and being the rock in unsteady times. We performed those tasks to the delight of our congregations. As a psychoanalyst, I am asking you to own that however noble your ministry was and is, it took a toll on you. Our professional life added to our level of stress. We need caregivers to care for us. I cannot write too many times the need for faith-based leaders to have a psychotherapist that you visit on a regular basis. Clergy need a safe space to process our feelings, thoughts, challenges, and our met and unmet needs.

Radicals believe that you cannot discuss character without a conversation about the courage to be prophetic. This book extends a call to be prophetic. My invitation is that you find it in your character to speak truth to power, advocate for the voiceless, stand up for the marginalized, and act on behalf of those who seek courageous leadership, be it the challenges of a triple pandemic, fighting for a stop sign, or protests against police brutality. The challenges may change but the need for prophetic action is a constant. Such work is stressful. Use your caregivers to monitor what the work is doing to your mind, body, and spirit.

### Listen to Your Symptoms

- Feelings of depression (sadness, hopelessness, mood swings, negative attitude/affect)
- Feelings of emotional exhaustion
- Feeling overwhelmed
- Observable behavioral changes (irritability, isolation, mood changes, nightmares)
- Decreasing interest in work
- Decrease in work production
- Decrease in energy
- Withdrawal from social contacts

- Increased use of cigarettes, stimulants, drugs, and/or alcohol
- Increased fear of death
- Weight changes
- Sleep disturbances
- Loss or increase in appetite
- Feelings of helplessness
- Never-ending sense of fatigue
- Lack of appreciation
- Gastrointestinal disturbances
- Respiratory problems
- Frequent headaches
- Loss of enthusiasm
- Decreased frustration tolerance
- Apathy, emotional detachment, or boredom

The symptoms I listed are the ones that send faith-based leaders to visit a therapist. Left unchecked, those symptoms sometimes send you to the hospital or worse. If we learned nothing else from the horrors of the COVID-19 pandemic, we learned that no change in one's health is insignificant. Do not ignore symptoms. Please do not be so busy saving the world that you have no time to see a healthcare provider. It is a matter of life or death.

### Live Smart

Given the vocational demands that clergy face and the realities of the Stressful Six mentioned on page 135, to "Live Smart" is an invitation to pay attention to self-care. Our body speaks. The challenge is to listen and be responsive to what our body is saying.

- Listen to your body, mind, and spirit. Get a checkup. Check out your nutritional habits.
- Set realistic goals and develop clear boundaries.

- Learn how to let go, and learn how to say, "No!"
- Learn relaxation techniques.
- Take care of your health.
- Insist on private time.
- Maintain a life outside of your caregiver role. Live a balanced life.
- Take time to play.
- Be accountable. Who mentors you? Who corrects you and cares for you?
- Know your limitations. What are your strengths and weaknesses?
- Keep a sense of humor. Have fun!
- Seek professional help. Workshops, counselors, retreat centers, massages, etc.
- Seek spiritual renewal. Read, pray, meditate, sing, keep a spiritual journal, worship.
- Engage in cardiovascular, aerobic exercise for at least thirty minutes, five days a week.
- Adopt an attitude of gratitude. Give thanks daily.
- Respect others and show them your appreciation.
- Walk your talk. Live a life congruent with your values.
- Love yourself. Love and be loved. Learn your love language.
- View failures and obstacles as learning experiences or feedback.
- Establish your priorities. Write your own script.
- Develop time and life management skills.
- Avoid negative or destructive thoughts as often as humanly possible.
- Avoid negative people as often as you can.
- Learn how to manage stress.
- Keep a daily log of your thoughts, feelings, reactions, questions, and key facts.
- Find a hobby. Learn how to decompress. Read, draw, paint, listen to or play music, visit a museum, see a play, go to the movies, go for a nature walk, do nothing, rest.

Over thirty years this one paragraph that I developed kept me sane: Expect Human Problems; Exercise Holy Practices and Engage Heaven's Power. In Times of Pressure; In Times of Pain; In Times of Pity; In Times of Pleasure: Manage Your Fear; Maintain Your Focus; and Maximize Your Faith; Examine Your Conduct; Explore Your Convictions; and Embrace Your Christ; We Operate Under Grace Not Guilt.

**Words of Wisdom from Dr. Frederick G. Sampson**

Dr. Frederick G. Sampson was a well-respected pastor, leader, and social justice advocate. After his death, his daughter put together a beautiful book[1] to journey through the life and ministry of this incredible man. He was one of my mentors and a close friend. We shared many meals together over a fourteen-year period. During our conversations over a meal, he offered me words of wisdom. Listed below is his rubric to read the temperature of society and offer hope.

The Mode of the Culture: Tension; Terror; Turbulence; and Trickery

The Method of Civilization: Intimidation; Manipulation; Domination; Isolation and Alienation

The Manner of the Church: Right Founder; Foundation; Fundamentals; Family; Function

In addition to the words of wisdom from Dr. Sampson I found this resource to be of help. Often in our mealtime conversations, Dr. Sampson connected biblical truths to mental health and clergy woundedness. My takeaway was we witness while wounded. Affirmation of this reality was found in the book *The Wounded Storyteller: Body, Illness and Ethics*, Second Edition by Arthur W. Frank.

**Leave a Legacy**

Joyce Hollyday of *Sojourners* magazine authored a book that you must include in your library: *Clothed with the Sun: Biblical Women, Social Justice, and Us*.[2] Hollyday makes a profound point in the chapter entitled "Used by a King." She notes that in the David and Bathsheba narrative, preachers and commentators tend to focus on King David's great sin rather than Bathsheba's great loss.[3] What parts of your story will be remembered or interpreted and by whom for what purpose?

How will history remember you? How will your life be summarized? The reality is that every life leaves a legacy; that is not an option. The question is, "What type of legacy do you want to leave?" However you frame that question, the truth is that you are working right now on the legacy you are going to leave.

## New Rules for Radicals: TNT for Faith-Based Leaders

Howard Thurman, a great thinker with Boston University roots, authored a book entitled *Jesus and the Disinherited*.[4] Thurman cautioned his readers to watch out for fear, deception, and hate. To do ministry, we must constantly guard against all three.

My prayer is these eight chapters helped you in your quest to engage in how best to serve humanity. Being a new radical is a process. It is not one mass march, only a few meetings, or a few headlines in the media. It is a lifestyle and commitment. The chapters were intended to walk you through a process. It is not necessarily linear, but following the steps outlined in the book may prove to be the most fruitful approach.

## NOTES

1. Freda Sampson, "I Think I Said Something. . ." The Life, Legacy & Ministry of Rev. Dr. Frederick G. Sampson, II (Detroit: Vision Publishing, LLC, 2018).

2. Joyce Hollyday, *Clothed with the Sun: Biblical Women, Social Justice, and Us* (Louisville, KY: Westminster John Knox Press, 1994).

3. Hollyday, 73.

4. Howard Thurman, *Jesus and the Disinherited* (Boston: Beacon Press, 1996; New York: Abingdon-Cokesbury Press, 1949).

# AFTERWORD

The Rev. Dr. Willard Ashley Sr. grew up in the same neighborhood where I spent my infancy being raised by an incredible woman of Puerto Rican heritage—New York City's Washington Heights neighborhood. Our paths crossed again as adults, when Will and I would pass each other in the hallway of the building I lived in and where he had several friends. We would often stop, talk, and share a laugh.

I don't believe in coincidences, so I believe these chance meetings were a foretelling of our future work together. After the tragedy of 9/11, Will was tasked by the National Council of Churches with supporting and healing clergy who were feeling traumatized and burned out by their work in helping their congregations and others through one of the most difficult times in American history. Will asked me to join him in this undertaking, and I can honestly tell you that he and his team made a real difference and a lasting impact on how clergy attend to crises while also engaging in self-care at the same time, in order to sustain effective leadership. Since that time, Will and I have remained great friends and worked together on several community projects. Also, I recently contributed a chapter to one of his previous books, *Learning to Lead: Lessons in Leadership for People of Faith*.

So now, given this significant moment in our history—experiencing a once-in-a-lifetime, earth-shattering pandemic—it is of little surprise that my friend Will would write *New Rules for Radicals: TNT for Faith-Based Leaders*, truly a book for our times. Each page reflects the man and his experiences as a Catholic kid from Harlem who turned into a Black Baptist pastor that power brokers cannot ignore.

Early in his life, Willard Ashley was the vice president of the Youth Division of the Harlem branch of the NAACP. He was preparing his life's work as an advocate, a fierce fighter for justice, and a captivating orator. God taught young Will how to throw out opponents when he played both catcher and first base for the Braves of the Henry Hudson Little League and the 158th Street team at the Harlem YMCA.

The title of this book gave me pause because in this politically and racially divided country we call America, the word radical is not associated with civic-minded people who love their country. Will is firmly entrenched on the ethical, humanistic, and spiritual side of history as he provides a new definition of "radical," noting that he or she is one who "practices non-violent tactics to bring about social justice." He argues, "Radicals organize communities to engage in socially responsible actions to usher in sustainable changes to society." With this, all political parties and people of goodwill can exhale. Will does not bash the left or the right. Instead, he calls for the social disruption that leads to negotiation for a stronger society for ALL our citizens. In his own words, "Radicals play by a set of rules guided by sound spiritual practices that honor creation and the humanity in every person."

True to the guy I have watched and worked with through some of the most turbulent times in American and world history, in *New Rules for Radicals*, Will finds moments of humor as he faces danger, meets with world leaders, and plots how to win against overwhelming odds. The book is an inspiration, and each page is filled with hope. All citizens can relate to this book, especially if you ever felt shut out of the conversation about the future of your neighborhood, community, or country. As a media personality, professor, psychologist, father, and husband, I appreciate Will's transparency and honesty about the dangers, costs, and realities of standing up for justice. He does not paint a naïve picture of community organizing as a cakewalk. Instead, with great care and proficiency, the book highlights the harmful reactions that may come from challenging the status quo. Will affirms the effective use of "charisma" as a God-given gift that one can use to the benefit of the community and the causes that one holds dear.

Will uses his skills as a psychoanalyst, pastor, and professor to dive into the temperament, mindset, and spiritual grounding necessary to engage in battles against status quo thinking, and he outlines the steps needed to bring about effective change. He admittedly owns that there are radical souls who make mountains out of what others may deem as molehills. He points to the Old Testament prophets as examples of leaders who approach evil and injustice with razor-sharp precision and holy rage. He also cautions that this work is not for those who lack courage or fear losing cozy relationships with the government, business, or influential people.

Over the years, I've known Willard Ashley to be someone who practices what he preaches about standing up for right. In that regard, *New Rules for Radicals* is a welcome departure from theoretical debates, as Will offers the reader a practical, insider's view of political chess games and how to win for the people. We are all the better because he found time to reflect and write about his many battles, victories, and lessons learned in the fight for justice. We can increase our understanding of how change occurs in neighborhoods and systems from reading this book.

To you, Will, my friend and my brother, please continue fighting. Keep reminding us to never give up the battle for what is right, fair, and just for all citizens. May this book give your readers the tools, strength, and energy to seek justice because until all of us are free, none of us can be free.

Jeffrey R. Gardere, MPhil, MS, DMin,  PhD, ABPP
Board Certified Clinical Psychologist
Associate Professor
Touro College of Osteopathic Medicine

# ADDITIONAL RESOURCES

Agosto, Efrain. *Servant Leadership: Jesus and Paul*. St. Louis: Chalice Press, 2005.

Ashley, Willard W. C., Sr., ed. *Learning to Lead: Lessons in Leadership for People of Faith*. Woodstock, NY: Skylight Paths Publishing, 2013.

Cross, Tiffany D. *Say It Louder: Black Voters, White Narratives, and Saving Our Democracy*. New York: Harper Collins, 2020.

Cutler, Alan. *Leadership Psychology: How the Best Leaders Inspire Their People*. London: Kogan Page, 2014.

Garrido, Ann. *Redeeming Conflict: 12 Habits for Christian Leaders*. Notre Dame, IN: Ave Maria Press, 2016.

Goza, Joel Edward. *America's Unholy Ghosts: The Racist Roots of Our Faith and Politics*. Eugene, OR: Cascade Books, 2019.

Gutheil, Thomas G. and Eric Y. Drogin. *The Mental Health Professional in Court: A Survival Guide*. Arlington, VA: American Psychiatric Publishing, 2013.

Hattery, Angela and Earl Smith. *Policing Black Bodies: How Black Lives Are Surveilled and How to Work for Change*. Lanham, MD: Rowman and Littlefield, 2018.

Heifetz, Ronald, and Marty Linsky. *Leadership on the Line: Staying Alive through the Dangers of Change*. Boston: Harvard Business Review Press, 2002.

HRSA Data Warehouse. "Find a Health Center." U.S. Department of Health and Human Services. https://findahealthcenter.hrsa.gov/.

Lear, Jonathan. *Radical Hope: Ethics in the Face of Cultural Devastation*. Cambridge, MA: Harvard University Press, 2006.

McKinney, Lora-Ellen. *Getting to Amen: 8 Strategies*

*for Managing Conflict in the African American Church.*
Valley Forge, PA: Judson Press, 2005.

National Center for Complementary and Integrative
Medicine. "What Does NCCIH Do?" National Institutes
of Health. https://nccih.nih.gov/.

Oswald, Roy and Arland Jacobson. *The Emotional
Intelligence of Jesus: Relational Smarts for Religious
Leaders.* Lanham, MD: Rowman and Littlefield, 2015.

Substance Abuse and Mental Health Services Administration. "Find Treatment." https://www.samhsa.gov/
find-help.

U.S. Department of Agriculture. "My Plate." https://
www.choosemyplate.gov/.

Washington, Harriet A. *A Terrible Thing to Waste:
Environmental Racism and Its Assault on the American
Mind.* New York: Little, Brown Spark, 2019.